Publishers:
Complete Self-Protection
www.CompleteSelfProtection.com

Photographs:
TP Photography
Tony.papps@btinternet.com
http://papps.smugmug.com

Copy-Editing and Typesetting:
WordsWay Copyediting
dhirenbahl@vsnl.com
www.wordsway.com

Printed and bound in Great Britain by J. H. Haynes & Co. Ltd.

A CIP Catalogue for this book is available from the British Library.


ISBN 978-0-9560031-0-2

# FENCE CONCEPTS

## The Most Powerful Self-Protection Tool

### AL PEASLAND

Complete Self-Protection

To my wonderful parents, who have shown
nothing but everlasting support for all that
I've done and achieved

With all my love,
Always,
Al

# Contents

About the Author                                    i

Foreword                                            1

Acknowledgements                                    4

Introduction                                        7

What is the 'Fence'?                               12

Types of Fence                                     23

Passive Fence                                      28

Controlling Fence                                  37

Submissive Fence                                   45

Aggressive Fence                                   50

Playing the Situation Down                         60

Playing the Situation Up                           64

Attacks From the Fence                             67

Common Mistakes                                    83

Action Triggers                                    89

What is Fear? The Effects of Adrenalin             91

Fear: Controlling Your Own Fears                   97

Know Your Enemy                                    104

The Fence and the Law                             110

How to Escape                                      114

Training the Fence                                120

Epilogue                                          127

# About the Author

With over 20 years of martial arts training, Al Peasland is the most experienced instructor in the Geoff Thompson Real Combat System (RCS) and is recognised as one of the pioneering members of RCS, acting as Geoff's personal uke on a daily basis during the system's most pivotal and developmental years.

Highly regarded amongst his peers for his technical ability and attention to detail, Al is also a veteran of literally hundreds of Animal Day fights, which were the controversial and much-publicised no-holds-barred fighting sessions in the late 1990s.

Al has also worked for many years as a nightclub doorman in Coventry, when the city was polled as the most violent in Europe for its size and population, and it was during this time that he developed his own Complete Self-Protection system that proved so successful during many violent and potentially life-threatening situations.

Whilst Al is trained and highly qualified in all ranges of unarmed combat, Al's speciality is an articulation and gentleness combined with a great fighting tenacity that is quite rare both in and out of martial arts circles.

Currently, Al is training and teaching his own Complete Self-Protection (CSP) system , which is fully recognised by the British Combat Association (BCA), in addition to acting as an assistant instructor on the Geoff Thompson Master Class seminars.

With Complete Self-Protection, Al is very aware that self-protection skills should be available to all members of society and not just to those already practising one of the martial arts systems. Whilst protecting oneself against a physical attack is a big part of self-protection and physical training, Al believes that gaining the skills to protect ourselves from ourselves and developing a strong character that will enable us to lead more fulfilling lives is of prime importance. It is this courage and self-understanding that will enable us to chase our dreams and realise our true potential.

Al has trained with some of the world's leading instructors in each of their own arts, and as a result has amassed an impressive array of qualifications that he now brings to his own CSP system, including:

- 4th Dan Senior Instructor with the BCA (British Combat Association)
- 3rd Dan Karate with CEKA affiliated to JKA
- 1st Dan Shotokan Karate with KUGB
- 1st Dan Sambo Russian Wrestling
- ABA Assistant Boxing Coach
- Freestyle Wrestling Coach
- Greco-Roman Wrestling Coach
- Qualified Close Protection Operative (Peter Consterdine Chase Consultants)
- Geoff Thompson Animal Day Veteran

# Foreword

## Geoff Thompson

The great thing about placing yourself in a very violent arena is that you learn reliable survival techniques very quickly.

You simply have to.

There is no room in reality for hypotheses; technique is either effective or you end up on a stretcher at the A&E, or worse still, a slab at the mortuary.

It has happened. It happens. Unfortunately, it will happen again.

People die in violent altercations you know!

That's what I did...(no I didn't die!) I placed my bones into the ultimate arena to see if my technique passed the acid test. Actually, it was more drastic than that: I entered the pavement arena to see if I passed the ultimate acid test.

Fortunately, I did (pass). Mostly because I adapted and forged myself and my technique to accommodate an arena that was as savage as it was unrelenting.

I learned many things during that time: that pre-emption was the only consistently effective physical technique; blocks, counters and traps are useless; intention is all-powerful; and violence is ultimately futile.

I also learnt that all the prolifically effective fighters I met had one thing in common: they all used the Fence as the controlling factor between them and an adversary. They didn't call it the 'Fence', of course (that was my job); in fact, most of them were not even aware that they were using a fence. What they had developed was both unconscious and innate, perhaps the by-product of facing severe and prolonged physical threat.

Many years later, when I started teaching survival techniques, the Fence was a critical part of my curriculum, and even though it was hardly known back then, it soon caught on.

Now it's hard to pick up a martial arts magazine without tripping over a photo-shoot of someone doing the Fence (in their own inimitable way).

This is both pleasing and slightly unsettling.

Pleasing, because I know that (conceptually) the Fence first found life in Coventry, England. More specifically, the term was coined at my own martial arts club where a small group of dedicated folk hungry for some combative honesty gave birth to a whole new era of reality training.

Unsettling (ever so slightly), because most of what I see in the martial arts arena today does not really represent the Fence that I conceived, wrote about and taught. It offers instead a poor watered-down facsimile of the real thing.

The Fence is a technique that could one day – if learned and practised diligently – save your life. To me it is (nothing less than) my front line in any potentially violent altercation. It allows me to control that all-important gap between myself and my potential assailant.

As we all should know, if you control the gap, you control the fight.

And now I am delighted to say, at 20 years of age, the Fence is about to be reborn, this time in the guise of an excellent book/ DVD combination produced by Al Peasland, my uke, my brother, my very close friend. And I couldn't be happier. Not only has Al committed his vast and practically unequalled knowledge to print, he has done what any good pioneer should do: he has gone out into the world and first tested it for himself. This, then, is not a book that simply copies what has been written and told before. Al took the knowledge he gained from me in thousands of hours of blood-and-snot instruction and subjected it to seven years of pressure-testing on the nightclub doors of a city (Coventry) that was once polled as being the most violent in Europe for its size and population.

That is why this book is important.

It is why I endorse it.

It is why this book may at some time prove life-saving.

This is a great read, the most comprehensive book on the Fence in the world today.

Read it, learn from it, and make it your own.

17 June 2008                                    Geoff Thompson
Coventry, England

# Acknowledgements

My martial arts career has now exceeded 22 years. Yes, it's true: I started before I was even born.

Well, actually I started my very first martial arts training session at the tender age of 12. Before then, all I had done was watch lots and lots of Bruce Lee and Chuck Norris films and practised flying kicks off my bed, much to the annoyance of my mum and dad who would put up with the constant thuds coming from above the living room until they could stand it no longer.

I don't want this chapter to read like a tedious awards ceremony speech where I start by thanking my manager and finish by crediting it all to God, but there are a few people whom I would like to take this opportunity to send a special thank you to.

You have my permission to skip to the next chapter if back-slapping, tear-jerking narrations aren't your thing.

I firstly must thank my parents for encouraging my sister and me to try out the local karate club – if only to save the bedsprings and floorboards in my bedroom from any further double-spinning, jumping back-kick punishment.

My biggest thanks have to go to my brother (actually, brother-in-law) Geoff Thompson.

Although I didn't know it, I was blessed to find out that the karate club nearest to my home was the Shotokan Club run by Geoff.

It just goes to show how sometimes fate steps in and what appears to be a simple decision can have a life-changing and lasting effect.

The only reason I chose Geoff's club was because of it's proximity to my home. I often look back and wonder where I would be now if I hadn't chosen that club, as I'm sure does my sister – who later became Mrs Geoff Thompson.

Geoff is without doubt the man who has shaped me the most during my formative years, my biggest influence and my biggest role model.

It was Geoff who gave me the toughest training sessions to build me up, not break me down, although I did question the motives of the constant KOs (knock-outs) on our Sunday sessions and the resulting slurred speech on the Monday mornings. I know now that it was all for a reason, one which has most definitely saved my life in the years following.

It was Geoff who also introduced me to many other great martial arts, by selflessly encouraging me to train with some of the best practitioners of these arts as well as bringing them to my doorstep in order to train me.

Geoff introduced me to doorwork, after I had spent several years standing with him as a young 16-year-old, meeting all the amazingly colourful characters that that world has to offer and watching some of the best doormen I have ever met ply their trade with pure professionalism.

It was during my first years on the door, where I had to grow at a rate of knots in order to handle this unique and dangerous profession, that I was also Geoff's primary daily training partner. It is without question that during my late teens and early 20s I developed most as a martial artist and honed my own skills in the direction of what really works and what really doesn't in live situations that are far removed from the safety and security of the dojo or gym.

I can honestly say that I would not be walking this lovely planet today if it wasn't for the training, the confidence, the life skills and the support of my brother-in-law, Geoff. Some of those skills I now try to pass on to you in this manual.

I've trained with lots of amazing people over the years and it would be wrong of me to try to list them all here, for fear that I may forget one or two. But all those who know me, will know I value the time we spent together on the mat and on the door and cherish their friendship.

I must also thank my sister Sharon. Not only for protecting me in a 'Big Sister' routine during all those hard karate sessions, but also for being a constant support and for showing me unconditional and non-judgemental love. It is with her encouragement and that of a few other very close friends that this book has made it this far, and hopefully will be the starter of many more to come.

Thanks to Mick for being a constant friend and support. I also have to say that I am still roaming this spinning globe because of his friendship, a brotherly friendship that has carried me through a battle far different to any I'd experienced before.

I am here, in this form, because of these and other close friends. This book is for you and because of you.

Love,
Al

# Introduction

For those who don't know me, I think this is probably as good a time as any to give you a brief background and résumé of my career to date.

I started training in Shotokan Karate at the age of 12. I'm sure those involved at the time will support me in this when I say I don't think I had seen before or have seen since a tougher traditional karate club than our little club in Longford, Coventry.

Under the guidance of Geoff Thompson, I reached 1st Dan with the KUGB and then progressed to 3rd Dan under the CEKA, an association run by another amazing karate international, Ian McCranor.

During this time we experimented massively with other styles and arts as a by-product of Geoff's own search for what worked and what didn't in the Real World.

It was this search which formed the basis for Geoff's own style of Real Combat System and indeed my own Complete Self-Protection concepts.

I quickly got into boxing and achieved my Assistant ABA coaching qualification. I then gained instructor-level status in both Greco-Roman and Freestyle wrestling under the tutelage of Khris Whelan in Manchester.

As the profile of our club and our now infamous Animal Day sessions grew, we found we attracted other great martial artists into our world. One of them was Vladim Kolganov (Van) who helped Geoff and I gain our 1st Dan qualifications in Sambo Russian Wrestling.

My CV reads very much like that of a wrestler who's done a bit of karate, and while I haven't donned my karate *gi* in many years, I will always consider myself a karateka. It is where I started, and an art that I will always love, regardless of which school of thought you are in when it comes to its effectiveness in real situations.

Whilst some of the techniques are not that applicable, it was the way we trained the art, the discipline I gained as a young impressionable karateka, the toughness and strength of will that the physically-punishing training regime developed that has helped me achieve my modest level of success in the real world.

I owe an awful lot to my early karate days, as much as I do all of the other arts that I have learned and merged into the one system that I have found to work very well for me.

I moved into doorwork at the age of 18. I started work for and with one of my best friends now, Clive. I would have to say that what I got from my training in terms of real physical self-protection skills, Clive gave me the same education in human behaviour and psychology skills – which took me from being a tough but incredibly naïve 18-year-old to a very street-savvy 19-year-old.

Without Clive watching my back I doubt I would be here now, certainly not with my good looks still intact (no comments please!)

Although Clive has never done a day's physical combative training in his life (as far as I'm aware), I was never in any doubt he was with me regardless of the odds. It was this attitude, determination and aggressive confidence that I too developed by watching Clive and others around me at the time.

In total I have now spent 22 years training in various martial arts covering punching, kicking and grappling arts.

I spent roughly seven of those years working full-time on Coventry's dangerous and violent streets as a pub and nightclub doorman, where I evolved my own concepts for self-protection.

It's fair to say that if you watch me train and teach now, I have pretty much the same message as that of my contemporaries (Geoff Thompson, Matty Evans, Tony Somers, etc.), but then, if what we're doing really does work, because we've all tested it and proved it works for real, then the message is always going to be the same and I make no apologies for that.

The last thing I am going to do in this book is elaborate and embellish what is typically a simple system for controlling violent confrontations and finishing quickly either with or without physical intervention.

To add to this concept for the purposes of making a 'full syllabus' would be wrong on my part as an instructor and coach, and any 'reality-based' system that does anything to take the message away from that of a very simple and basic one has missed the point, in my humble opinion.

I can categorically say that I do not think I would be here to pen these words now if it wasn't for some of the techniques listed in this manual. They have not only been tested in very real situations by myself, but also by the man who brought these concepts to the forefront quite some years ago, Geoff Thompson.

Geoff certainly doesn't claim to have invented these techniques and concepts, but he most definitely was the person who raised the profile and made us all aware that there is a huge fighting/self-protection range to be learned in the pre-fight arena. He also analysed in more detail the philosophies and strategies that he found to work with these techniques, something that I don't think had been done until that point.

First, I'd like to thank you for taking the time and trouble to acquire (hopefully purchase) and read this book.

I'd like to start by saying that the concepts within are merely my own interpretation and understanding of the theories and techniques of the 'Fence'. It is for everyone to find their own way and build their own 'castle'. I am merely giving you some building blocks and talking you through the plans to my own structure in the hope that it gives you a start and some inspiration.

Coined by my mentor Geoff Thompson, the 'Fence' was a way of describing the control and protection of your personal space, in just the same way we build fences around our homes and property. Sometimes these fences are very clear and very visible; sometimes they are not so obvious.

We often hear of police cordoning off areas when trouble has hit, or agriculture ministers creating exclusion zones when there is an outbreak of foot-and-mouth. These are all variations of Fence Concepts on a much larger scale – but can be treated in the same way.

The techniques of the Fence serve several purposes.

- They offer protection of your personal space, keeping out

uninvited guests, which ultimately maintains your own level of comfort and well-being.

- They offer a visible deterrent to those unwanted guests, who can see there is now something hindering their advancement into your personal space.
- They offer a detection system, in much the same way as passive infra-red sensors and motion detectors do on sophisticated alarm systems, where the intruder may feel he has closed the distance and ventured in unimpeded, but your own personal Fence alarm system has detected him and you are actually preparing your defence/counterattack/escape, etc.

In this book we will cover all aspects of the 'Fence' in what I have termed 'Fence Concepts'.

I will often refer to the aggressor, or attacker as *he/him*. This is merely to save time as my one-finger typing is not the speediest and otherwise, this book may not have reached the shelves until 2010.

I may also use alternative terms such as attacker, assailant, aggressor, or opponent, just to try to alleviate any boredom and keep you interested.

The Fence and its myriad concepts and applications should be an integral part of your training if you are truly training in what is becoming more and more commonly termed RBSD (Reality-Based Self-Defence).

If you are not training Fence Concepts, then you have missed what I believe to be the most important part of a good reality-based system.

By applying Fence Concepts effectively, you not only open up windows of opportunity for getting your first pre-emptive strike onto your opponent(s), but also give yourself a much better chance of assessing situations early, controlling situations, and also providing yourself with opportunities to escape.

The Fence gives you all the tools you need to apply effective awareness, avoidance, and escape tactics, which should always be your primary objective in every situation.

I would like to emphasise that, whilst this book will contain lots of techniques and methods to attack and injure your aggressor, *your first course of action should always be to escape.*

I state now and repeat later in this book that you should only hit and be pre-emptive when you are truly under threat, are truly in a dangerous situation, have exhausted all other avenues of escape, and when you feel your life and/or the lives of those around you are truly in danger.

In my opinion, should this genuinely be the case, then you are fully justified to hit first, hit hard, and not stop until the threat is over.

I do not mean you should continue hitting once the threat is no longer present – nor should you stop after the first punch to assess the effects and maybe even congratulate yourself on a good punch thrown. Stop when the aggressor is down and not posing any more threat to you.

In titles to be released soon, I will be discussing in more detail my own concepts on Pre-Emptive Striking, which will be a great supplement to this manual, but on its own, this manual will provide you with all the tools you need to equip yourself with an effective, efficient, and powerful Fence.

Finally, if the book seems a little slim, I make no apologies. I refuse to 'pad out' the material to make a more substantial-looking book. What is contained within has been tested thoroughly in high-pressure situations in and out of the gym.

I can say categorically that I have used, at one point or another, all the techniques detailed within and will stand by them as being effective in the specific situations they are designed for.

I thank you again for taking the time to read this manual and wish you all the best in your future training.

# What is the 'Fence'?

In very simple terms, the Fence is a system that allows you to control a potentially violent confrontation with an aggressor or aggressors before it actually becomes violent. It is an integral part of your self-protection arsenal and something you can carry with you all day every day in just the same way as you carry and employ your awareness and avoidance techniques.

If you are switched on and aware of your surroundings, your Fence offers you the added opportunity to control yourself in a situation; to control your aggressor both physically, mentally and emotionally and to allow you to take charge and so conclude the situation in whatever manner you wish.

We read a lot about how to effectively dispose of an attacker, with critiques on which techniques are the most effective at disabling, or knocking out, or incapacitating your aggressor when it gets physical.

We also read a lot about how we should always be aware of our surroundings, avoid potentially dangerous situations and locations, and always escape and remove ourselves from such situations the moment we become aware of them.

These are all valid and necessary parts of self-protection and where Fence Concepts fits in is the unique instance between awareness and avoidance, and the physical conflict stages.

In fact, it sits right in the middle.

If there's one thing I've realised in the many violent confrontations, and the very real situations that I have experienced working as a doorman, it's that nothing ever works as planned. Nothing is ever 'right' when it kicks off, and that we all make mistakes.

While I hope that I can spend the rest of my life employing effective awareness and avoidance skills, sometimes situations just grow past that and you quickly find yourself in a confrontation where you can no longer simply avoid or escape.

Working the door is a prime example because you simply can't leave your post: that is the very reason you are there in the first place, to deal with these violent individuals.

That is why working the door was a great learning and testing ground for the Fence Concepts because, by it's own nature, it created an environment that forced its use to control, override, defuse, and end potentially violent situations.

I agree that it is not exactly representative of real-life situations, because as individuals going about our ordinary lives we always have the option to avoid and escape. When it's your job to stay, that changes the dynamic.

However, what I do say is that doorwork forces you to use the Fence and its use effectively affords you an easier, less violent night.

So when our avoidance has either failed us or the situation has not allowed us to escape, then the Fence is what allows us to take control and mastery of the situation and offers us an opportunity to engage in dialogue with our aggressors, before physical action commences.

Due to the fact that we have this control over the situation, we are then able to either engineer an end to it with verbal techniques such as verbal dissuasion or aggressive posturing and language, or we can use it to give our physical action a better chance of success.

Before I proceed to talk about the Fence and it's variations, I first want to clarify a key part of self-protection, and that is 'colour coding'. Colour coding is a way of defining what level of awareness, alertness and defensive strategy we should employ based on perceived and known levels of potential and real threat.

We often hear this in the news on a much larger scale when the UK is put on Red Alert of a potential terrorist attack.

Colour coding works exactly the same way at a personal and individual level.

In my opinion, physical techniques are only a very small percentage of personal self-defence, the major part being awareness. With awareness you can identify, quantify, and then avoid potentially dangerous and violent situations. Without awareness you simply become an easy target, vulnerable to surprise attack and often finding yourself in troublesome situations without even realising it.

Colour coding is not my invention. It was originally developed by Col. Jeff Cooper, designed specifically for military use in order to differentiate different levels of awareness and threat assessment.

Fig. 1 highlights the four main colour codes, although there are others that will not be directly applicable to the application of Fence Concepts.

The colours help us to categorise the rising levels of threat and show us the actions we should all take at each state of awareness.

What I've included in Fig. 1 for future reference are the various Fence Concept principles and where they sit in with the levels of awareness and threat. We will be discussing these various principles later in this manual, so it is merely sufficient to highlight them and I suggest you refer back to this chart as you read on.

## Code White

Code White can be described as day-dreaming, or being 'switched off'.

It is not a place we want to be in if we are to offer ourselves any chance of spotting potential danger and being able to take the necessary action to avoid it before it escalates.

It is people in this condition that most attackers will seek and select: you are easy prey and more likely to be shocked by a sudden surprise attack, which is exactly what the attacker is looking for.

Activities such as talking on your mobile phone or reading a paper while walking around in public will result in your being distracted and move you into a Code White state.

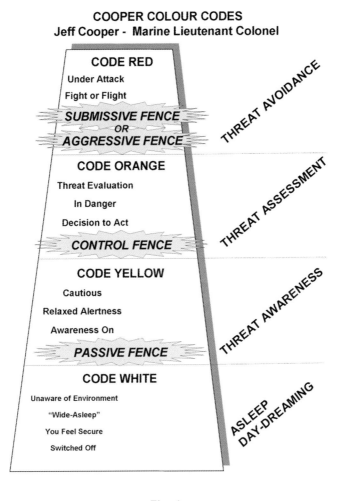

Fig. 1

The negative side effects of being in Code White are that:

- you feel secure, whether or not you are actually safe;
- your awareness is switched off; and
- you are unaware of your environment, its inhabitants, and their rituals of attack.

## Code Yellow

Code Yellow is where you should spend most of your time. In this state you are more alert, more aware of your surroundings and what is going on in your environment.

However, it is difficult to remain in this level of awareness for long and it can often be considered 'paranoid', but it is something that must be practised deliberately until it becomes a natural state.

You want this state of alertness to become as automatic and instinctive as tying your shoelaces, and this will only come if you actively train yourself to be cautious rather than remaining complacent.

The key points of Code Yellow are that:

- you are cautious;
- your awareness is switched on;
- you are aware of potential threat with a relaxed alertness; and
- you have increased peripheral awareness and are less likely to be surprised by attackers hiding in doorways, around corners, behind parked cars, etc.

## Code Orange

Code Orange is a heightened level of alertness, a result of a potential threat that you have spotted during your Code Yellow awareness.

You are now in a position where you have spotted a threat, perhaps a gang of hoodies loitering by a shop doorway or even simply a feeling that something isn't quite right.

This is decision time and you now have to decide how you are going to act and take charge of this situation rather than let it progress further without your control.

The key points of Code Orange are:

- you are in danger, and are aware of a potential threat;
- you now need to evaluate the level of this threat;
- a target has been identified so you are now in a specific alert state rather than being generally alert;
- assessment of your environment is critical, and you look for

escape routes; and
- you make a decision on your action.

## Code Red

If you are in Code Red then you are actually fighting or taking the action you have decided upon during Code Orange.

You are now in conflict and are having to make good your escape or end of the conflict by whatever means necessary, be it verbal dissuasion, or in the worst case, physical attack.

Thinking time is now over, and if you have failed in your earlier states of awareness to plan and prepare your appropriate action, then you will be left to run on autopilot, using whatever you have trained the most in.

This is without doubt the worst place to be and is to be avoided at all costs.

Anyone who has been there in a real-life physical encounter, particularly one that has resulted in physical attack, will concur that more effort should be spent working the earlier codes of awareness so that this level is hopefully never reached.

The key points of Code Red are:
- you are in conflict;
- this is fight-or-flight time; you should have already evaluated the level of threat and already made your decision over which course of action to take;
- escape must always be the first choice; and
- use of the appropriate level of force is essential.

## Applying the Colour Codes of Awareness

You should start right now to apply these colour codes of awareness.

Be analytical with yourself and correct yourself if you find that you are drifting into Code White at any time, even when at home.

The different states of awareness should be used on a sliding scale that you can scroll up and down during the course of your day. Look around your environment when walking along. Who is around you? If the person in front was to suddenly stop, what would you do? Are the roads busy? Could you quickly cross the road without putting yourself in further danger?

Experiment by moving yourself from Code Yellow to Orange deliberately by creating potential scenarios. Eventually, you won't have to think about this: it will become natural and will no longer feel like paranoia, just being prepared.

## Note to the Reader

Now, if you've just read this section and are already starting to think this book is about making us all highly-strung, paranoid individuals, afraid to leave our own homes because of danger on every street corner, please don't.

It is not my intention to turn everyone into quivering wrecks at the thought of leaving their front doors. We all need to lead balanced, relaxed and fun lives, and to do this we need to have a level of personal security that feels natural. The only way to get it to feel natural is to do it constantly.

For example, the action of putting our seat belts on before we drive off is now instinctive for most of us. However, if you remember back to when you first had to do this you would have been all fingers and thumbs, having to look down to the seat belt socket to plug in the clasp. Repetition of this task has made it a natural act, a second instinct, and one which offers you a great deal of passive protection should you be unfortunate enough to have an accident, and prefer not to greet your windscreen with your face.

Applying colour code principles whilst going about your everyday tasks is exactly the same. Practise it until it stops being a hindrance and uncomfortable and starts to become a natural, passive action that provides a safety net of security to help make your life's journey enjoyable and danger-free.

## The Fence Concepts Flowchart

The Fence Concepts Flowchart (Fig. 2) is a very rough guide of how I interpret the Fence Concepts and how, in a very generalised format, I expect a confrontational situation to evolve.

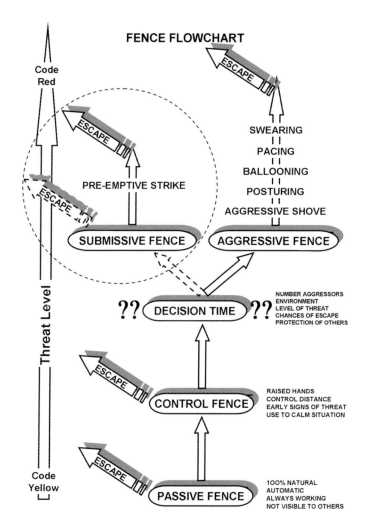

**Fig. 2**

I recommend you bookmark this page so that you can refer back to this chart as you progress through the rest of this manual.

You can see from the chart that we must all start out in a Passive Fence state. This is simply a physical version of what self-protection systems would call a mental state of Code Yellow or 'Aware'.

If a situation escalates and you need to take more control over it because you are not able to leave immediately, then just as your mental security state will move up to a Code Orange (start to take action), so your Fence moves up to a more visible controlling state.

At every stage we must consider escape, because every situation is different and if the opportunity arises to get away from the danger and the threat, then we should take it. This should be as big a part of your training as the pre-emptive strike and the support system training such as boxing, grappling, karate, etc.

Once you have a Controlling Fence, you are now in control of the situation and from there you can start to make decisions. These will be based on lots of factors, and we will look at those later in this manual, but your primary decision is on which direction to take the confrontation, Submissive or Aggressive.

I will state this now and repeat it throughout this book. My whole philosophy of Complete Self-Protection is to develop ability such that we become better people, people with less ego, people with more self-control, and people with more compassion for others; even those who wish us harm.

It is with this in mind that I would always, wherever possible, take a situation to the Aggressive Fence if I had the chance.

It is the Aggressive Fence which offers us the psychological ability to defuse the situation by 'bottling out' our aggressors and so removing the need to get physical.

However, no two situations are the same and lots of other factors will contribute to which way you should go, but my main aim should always be to end it without having to strike or fight.

To go with a Submissive Fence, in my experience, you are almost always destined to be hitting, and hitting very, very soon.

I can probably only recall on one hand the number of times I've gone down the submissive route in order to mask the delivery of my pre-emptive strike, only for the aggressor to back away and change their minds. It very rarely happens, so basically, if you go submissive, you'll be fighting.

From the aggressive option you can then take it to another level by adding extra concepts such as ballooning, posturing and aggressor isolation, attaching roles and duties to your aggressors back-up.

## Understanding Your Enemy

Probably the biggest part of the Fence is its ability to offer you a chance to get into the mind of your aggressor and affect his own state. Whether that is to add more adrenalin and fear to his already heightened state, or to switch him off and trigger a mild endorphin release in order to relax him and gain an advantage.

I'm no psychologist or NLP (Neuro-Linguistic Programming) practitioner, but what I do know is what has worked for me for real, so I have learned that certain actions on my part have a certain resultant affect on my aggressor.

I've also spent many years experimenting within my own training, things such as Animal Days, in order to better understand the effects of fear, adrenalin, and my own body's reactions to certain stimuli.

My natural reactions under fearful situations are no different from those of any other humans, and by understanding that, I can better understand how my aggressor is feeling and reacting.

In addition, by immersing myself for many years in such heightened states, I am better equipped at utilising and adapting the fear and adrenalin that I experience.

Cus D'Amato, Mike Tyson's boxing coach and guardian, said: 'The hero and the coward both feel the same thing, but the hero uses his fear, projects it onto his opponent, while the coward runs. It's the same thing, fear, but it's what you do with it that matters.'

In the following chapters of this manual we will take each stage of the Fence Concepts process and look at it in more detail.

We will also examine some of the other processes which run in parallel to the Fence Concepts, including fear and the effects of fear, both for ourselves and for our aggressors. We will look at the involvement of the law and your rights as an individual to protect yourself within the confines of the legal system. Further, we will look at ways to train these concepts both on your own and with like-minded training partners.

As always, we do all this so that we hopefully never have to use it in real life.

This is the comprehensive car insurance that we take out and hope we never have to cash in.

However, hopefully, by reading, digesting and then practising the concepts detailed in this manual you will have taken your third-party insurance, up through fire and theft, and on to fully comprehensive with no claims bonus protection all thrown in.

(Apologies: my analogies are always a little abstract, as you will note from the rest of this manual.)

# Types of Fence

As you've already noticed, my analogies aren't the greatest, but the best I can come up with for describing the different types of Fence, but it's a pretty obvious one really. It's where the name itself was derived from, but even the obvious things can sometimes use a little deeper thought and explanation, so here goes.

Imagine you wanted to protect your lovely home, a large home with big gardens all around. First, you may want to install some kind of system that passively detects unwanted visitors, maybe PIR (Passive Infra-Red) sensors and security lights, motion detectors, etc.

These are all types of security that are barely visible to onlookers

but can give you an early warning system for detecting undesirables. They are also working around the clock, 24/7. This is what your own Passive Fence should be. It should be undetectable to the surrounding public and working 24/7. It should be as natural and as automatic and subconscious an act as tying your shoelaces.

Now let's imagine that you want to put up a more visible deterrent, a bit of 'in-yer-face' security that categorically shouts 'Keep Out'.

This is where your Passive Fence should switch to becoming a Controlling Fence and is where the term the 'Fence' was originally derived from.

It's exactly the same as you would do with your home. You'd put up a big 6-ft or 8-ft fence all around your property and post signs saying 'Keep Out'. You may even back this up with some veiled threats of 'Trespassers will be Prosecuted' or 'Beware of the Dog'. But this is all just supporting controlling tactics to instil some element of doubt into the potential intruder's mind and make him hesitate and think before he takes the next course of action.

This fence won't stop the determined intruder, nor will it cause him any real harm to penetrate or climb over. However, what it does do is set up your own personal safe space, your own boundary, inside which both you and the intruder know action will be taken if that line is crossed.

You put a fence up around your house to ensure that anyone who climbs over it has done so with a particular intention in mind: after all, it's hard to 'accidentally' climb over a fence and enter someone's private property 'unintentionally'.

Your own Controlling Fence (Picture 1) should provide the same deterrent and the same level of security.

The ground rules should be clearly set when your own fence is raised so that anyone moving forward and trying to break it down or come through it will have a price to pay. Action will be taken. Trespassers will be prosecuted.

**Picture 1**

Referring back to the original Fence Concepts Flowchart at the beginning of this book, we are now at the decision point where we go either Submissive or Aggressive.

The Submissive Fence is not something we would usually do in the protection of our own home, because, by its nature, we are actually trying to entice the intruder in by simulating or exposing weakness.

To do this would mean deliberately leaving a weak point in the fence surrounding your home that acts as a beacon to all would-be night prowlers looking for a soft target.

We tend to turn our homes into fortresses to prevent and deter – very rarely do we make them appear especially vulnerable so that we can draw in the burglar and surprise him with an ambush, but that is exactly what we are doing.

So we'll bend my analogy a little for the purposes of this explanation (I told you I'm not great at analogies).

Imagine you did just this; imagine you removed a panel from your garden fence. Imagine you deliberately left a window ajar, put the house in darkness and made it look as though you were all out for the night, but then you hid behind the curtains with your bat, waiting for the burglar to enter. A classic (well, maybe in the films, perhaps) ambush attack on someone who had let his guard down, who had thought the house was vulnerable to attack, a house that had given up trying to be strong and impenetrable. In fact, as he sets foot across the threshold, all hell breaks loose.

This is your Submissive Fence (Picture 2).
You are deliberately feigning weakness in the hope it draws your opponent into your pre-emptive attack.

**Picture 2**

Silent alarms in banks and at jewellers' use a similar process where the alarm will have been raised, but not to the intruders or thieves. This relaxes them a little giving them the false impression that they have more time to gather their loot, when actually the police are assembling outside readying themselves for their exit with the cuffs ready and the riot van doors already open.

Finally, we have the Aggressive Fence (Picture 3), coupled with ballooning and posturing.

This would be similar to releasing a pack of hungry guard dogs out into your grounds inside the perimeter fence.

What you're doing now is saying to any would-be burglar, 'Come into my space and you'll get eaten.'

The aim is not to end up with a bunch of well-fed Rottweilers, but to further deter the burglars from entering your space, to make them want to move on and find a softer target.

This is the exact aim of your own Aggressive Fence.

You use this not to start trouble or escalate it further: rather, you use it to deter and to reinforce that if the aggressor continues to move forward and enter your space he's going to get torn to pieces. You need to become the snarling, growling, angry, foaming-at-the-mouth guard dog behind your fence. Believe me, no one wants to fight a monster.

Picture 3

And so, with a very convoluted analogy, this is how I would best describe the Fence and its primary constituent concepts.

There are lots more intricacies and nuances to the Fence and as we delve deeper into them throughout this book, you will realise that what appears to be a simple set of techniques is actually quite a complex system that affords you lots of benefits. However, just by grabbing the basic understanding of these four main Fence Concepts you are already on your way to growing your own self-protection system with an invaluable tool, and one that, in my opinion, is the most important tool in your arsenal.

## Passive Fence

*The best way to subdue an enemy is to find them another one.*

—Sun Tzu, *The Art of War*

The Passive Fence is a position that should appear perfectly natural to those around you, and should also feel completely natural to you.

It is effectively a low guard, with your hands very low, or even by

your sides. The Passive Fence is to help maintain your own comfortable personal space, whatever range that may be, for when threat levels are extremely low or even non-existent. I use this all the time, even when talking with friends. Consequently, it should be invisible to those around you on a conscious level and very, very natural.

Subconsciously, however, people, including potential attackers, will sense the air of confidence that backs up your positive posture and will often think twice before even starting trouble.

Try occupying your hands by playing with your wedding ring, or cufflinks (assuming you wear suits; not such a good look if you only wear T-shirts).

One stance that is a bit of a habit of mine is to stand and pick the calluses on the inside knuckles of my hand (Picture 4).

It's a great way to hide the fact that you are now standing with your hands in front of your body with a very low guard position, and because you can use this action to appear as though deeply engrossed in this activity, it also gives the impression of nonchalance and a relaxed attitude.

Sometimes it's useful to hide your alert state and feign ignorance of a threatening situation: this helps give you the element of surprise should you choose to take the Submissive and Pre-Emptive Strike course of action.

Although it should appear natural, that doesn't mean that your hands should be so relaxed that they are by your sides, offering you no protection at all, nor should they be raised too high so as to look out of place or unusual.

The Passive Fence takes time and effort to perfect and become comfortable with, but the more comfortable and familiar you are with positioning your hands in this manner, both when you are walking around and conversing with others, the less onlookers are likely to notice anything out of place at all.

When I'm standing still and conversing, another favourite position I adopt is what I call my Thinking Man's pose (Picture 5).

Picture 4                                        Picture 5

Here, I have my arms slightly folded with one hand pulling at my chin, as though in deep thought.

You often see people in this stance who have beards – particularly when they're tugging two-week-old food remnants from the undergrowth beneath their chin.

Either way, this is another great way to create a guard position, masked with the impression that your hands are there for another reason.

Again, the ability to appear deep in thought can help disguise your switched-on attitude beneath the surface, and I would also recommend using this type of Passive Fence when in close proximity with others, for example, when in confined or crowded spaces. Although being this close is not a great idea, you can still use it to your advantage, keeping your hands in a position that protects your body and your chin (Picture 6).

Picture 6                           Picture 7

Noisy bars and clubs also allow you to feign hardness of hearing, which, whilst getting you closer, also allows you to move off to the side and reduces your own target area a little (Picture 7).

Picture 8

It's my recommendation that you don't fully fold your arms: instead, merely cross them on your chest or belly, depending on your level of fitness and taste for tikka masalas (Picture 8). If the situation progresses rapidly and you need to react quickly, folded arms could slow you down when you need to get a shot off quickly (Pictures 9a and 9b).

In order to stay out of Code White and make Code Yellow a more normal and natural place to be in, the more likely you are to keep your Passive Fence alert and sensitive to danger.

Once you switch off and revert to Code White, your Passive Fence will switch off too.

A good way to practise the Passive Fence and also maintain a level of Code Yellow alertness is to use a technique that advanced

Picture 9a

Picture 9b

driving instructors teach, which is 'commentary driving'.

Commentary driving is basically talking while driving, and is a technique for improving many aspects of a driver's performance and in which the driver is required to keep up a running commentary of all hazards, actions, planning and observations whilst navigating around. A commentary could go something like this.

'Car turning right ahead …approaching roundabout check mirrors …reduce speed …change down to second …mirrors …clear …car overtaking in the left lane …second exit …', etc.

Getting over the embarrassment of talking out loud when there is nobody else in the car stops some people from bothering with the technique, but it must be done loudly for maximum effect. The reason that commentary driving works is that the driver hears gaps in his or her running commentary and these correspond to gaps in attentiveness.

This is a truly excellent technique which forces the driver to notice his own thoughts (or lack of them) whilst driving and is now acknowledged as a major cause of increased in-car safety.

So to adapt and apply this technique to walking around as opposed to driving, we develop the skills and the familiarity with staying in a Code Yellow state, which gradually becomes a normal state to be in.

I wouldn't recommend talking out loud whilst walking around the town shopping – you may find yourself becoming the interest of people in white coats – but you should certainly consider trying it by mentally thinking of all the dangers, hazards, concerns, observations, plans, that you will make as you walk around.

By staying alert you will afford yourself the chance of keeping your Passive Fence alert: after all, passive alarms are great, still, they only work if they are switched on and positioned correctly.

Correct positioning is vital and even when your Fence is a passive one, it's important to use your body language and gesturing to control the safe space in front of and around you (Picture 10).

Everyone has their own personal space, a space around them which feels comfortable.

When someone gets inside that space without your personal invite, it can feel uncomfortable, and this intuition plays a big part and can be a great indicator that someone or something is dangerously close.

Everyone's personal space is different. For example, I have one friend who likes to be very close when he talks to you, almost

Picture 10                              Picture 11

as though he's always going to tell you a secret. But it still feels uncomfortable for me to be that close: he's a friend, but not *that* good a friend, you understand.

So I use my Passive Fence as a way of increasing the gap between us to something that is more comfortable for me, and I do this by allowing my hands to gesture slightly more when I talk. By doing this, I make space for myself to be animated, but also satisfy his need to feel close by allowing my hands to stay within his personal space but the rest of my body outside.

When the situation is more real with a potential risk element, then the dangers of being too close can be more extreme (Picture 11).

By allowing the potential aggressor to come too close you start to leave vital targets within his range. It also leaves you less time to react should the situation escalate ahead of time, and at the same time reduces your ability to see what's happening around you.

Some examples of the classic types of attack you are vulnerable to include punches, close-range head-butts, and potentially even knife attacks (Picture 12).

Picture 12                        Picture 13

The problem with being too close is that it limits what you can see going on around you, and also what your aggressor is doing. His hands may be hidden, and it makes it very easy for him to throw a surprise attack, particularly with bladed weapons, which obviously need less speed and force to deliver deadly injuries.

Just as I'm no NLP guru, nor am I a knife expert, and have only dealt with knife attacks on a couple of occasions, but I do know that a good knife player will keep the weapon hidden and only need the weight of the blade to inflict serious injury.

The first you know will be the feeling of a punch in your side or a warm, wet feeling as the blood oozes from your body (Picture 13).

In close protection, there's a saying, taught to me by Peter Consterdine, that you must not be surprised by your vehicle.

That doesn't mean always being on your guard in case your Citroen C5 decides to jump up on your drive, turn itself into a robot humanoid and start busting some moves down your cul-de-sac when you're least expecting it.

What it does mean is that when you park your vehicle in a car park or street, never go for the easy/lazy option of parking as close to the stairwell or exit as you can.

It may be more convenient, but when returning to your car, you have less time and visibility around your vehicle to assess any potential threats.

While I've digressed slightly, the same goes for distancing when using the Passive Fence, and also the other variations of Fence discussed later.

You will already be starting to experience the narrowing of your peripheral vision, side effects of the adrenalin which will slowly be increasing in your body as the potential threat is realised.

The closer you stand to your prime aggressor, the less you can see to your sides and around him.

You will start to miss people and movement in your periphery that are also potential threats, simply because you are too close and too focussed on the one person in front of you.

Keeping a more comfortable distance allows you to better assess threats around you. It is often the case that the first punch will not be thrown by the prime aggressor but by one of his less courageous scumbag friends from the side, so keep this in mind.

I had a particularly nasty incident one evening working the door where I was attacked from my blind side whilst ejecting two other individuals who were still trying to fight each other.

Although I did have my hands full at the time with these two individuals, I was obviously too target-focused on their activities and had let my own peripheral vision and spatial awareness drop. This gave the third individual an opportunity to throw some heavy shots in the direction of my head, which I was fortunate enough to block with my face. (I don't remember that particular defence technique being taught in my karate syllabus, but I worked it well nonetheless.)

Sadly, this guy had spent too much time pushing weights and not enough hitting a heavy bag, so didn't manage to put me away, and he was eventually subdued with a rear choke, the technique for which will be covered in a separate instruction manual. But the story could have been a lot different if he'd been able to punch better.

So the importance of being able to see what is going on around you is vital, even when you are engaged with one or more primary aggressor.

In summary, the Passive Fence should:
- be 100 per cent natural;
- always be active;
- be automatic and instinctive;
- keep you switched-on and in Code Yellow;
- allow you to detect a potential threat early on; and
- afford you the opportunity to escape.

## Controlling Fence

*Therefore those skilled in war bring the enemy to the field of battle and are not brought there by him.*
—Sun Tzu, *The Art of War*

When you feel and sense that the situation is escalating and you need to raise your guard a little, this is when you progress to a Controlling Fence.

If the threat level increases, then you should make the conscious decision to take charge of the situation and gain control over your own personal safe space and also that of your aggressor, from both the physical and psychological points of view.

To refer back to the colour code diagram, this is where we move up to Code Orange, where we've now identified a threat, and where we're in a decision-making mode as to how to proceed and act to either avoid the threat or eliminate it.

This can often be misread and misinterpreted as a static position, similar to a more traditional karate stance where the master steps back with a forceful *gedanbarai* (lead arm low block), nor is it a forceful boxer's stance with the guard raised high, or any variation in between.

To make any such move will alert the aggressor to your intention that you are preparing for battle - and this is not the message we want to send out.

He'll also probably think you're an idiot and will relish the opportunity of destroying a completely naïve martial artist who has no clue of street fighting.

Your Controlling Fence should be strong but without it growing into an aggressive stance. At this stage, you have not given any indication as to whether you are going to go submissive or aggressive. Your outward body language should still appear to be non-committal where you have not decided which approach to take, whilst inwardly you should be completely focused on controlling the situation, maintaining distance, and analysing everything which will influence your next move.

Picture 14a

Picture 14b

Picture 14c

As I said, this is not a static position, which is always difficult to explain clearly with pictures in books. It should be fluid and mobile, but always be careful not to drop your hands down in an effort to move your Controlling Fence around (Pictures 14a, 14b, and 14c).

Some options are shown in Pictures 15a and 15b. Palms facing upwards or downwards are preferred for a Controlling Fence.

Picture 15a

Picture 15b

Picture 16a

Picture 16b

If your palms are facing forwards towards the aggressor, this will be seen as submissive body language (which we will cover in the next section).

We don't want to appear either aggressive or submissive; we are simply trying to take control of the situation and assert ourselves to manage our own personal space and allow us an extra bit of time to plan our next steps.

Alternative positions include staggering your hand positions. This also allows you to move into a short-stance position, obviously better from which to deliver your first shot, but slightly more noticeable, so care must be taken when adopting this position that the movement into a 'stance' isn't too obvious (Pictures 16a and 16b).

There is a big difference between being controlling and being aggressive, and it is this skill that you need to drill in training in order to establish where that line is.

You should still be talking with your hands and you should be able to maintain the gap between yourself and the aggressor (Pictures 17a and 17b).

Picture 17a                                    Picture 17b

The primary difference with the Controlling Fence as opposed to the Passive Fence is cleverly pointed out in the name. It does what it says on the tin, and should be used to gain control over the situation, even if that means gaining physical control.

While I'm in favour of attacking first and not waiting to be attacked, sometimes you are not quick enough or don't read the situation well enough, and this is when a good Controlling Fence can still afford you the option of trapping or hindering any sudden attack from the aggressor, such as jamming the attacking arm, either at the wrist or bicep.

This works particularly well from a Staggered Fence (Pictures 18a, 18b, and 18c).

Picture 18a

Picture 18b

Picture 18c

What I particularly like about the Controlling Fence is the ability to use tactile control and assess the reactions and intentions of the aggressor using physical sensitivity techniques.

This isn't applicable to all situations and must be used with some care, as often, reaching out to touch the aggressor holds a real danger of triggering an aggressive reaction in him.

However, if you can disguise these moves by your dialogue, then the

Picture 19                          Picture 20

act of touching your aggressor can be camouflaged (Picture 19).

I have friends who like to use the Staggered Fence to touch the lead arm, as if in a handshake position, and also to touch the aggressor's rear arm (Picture 20), either at the forearm position or higher up on the back of their triceps.

This is done very much in the way of a friendly pat, as if trying to make friends and showing softness on your part. It should not be an aggressive move, nor should it be too sudden.

The main aim is to see what kind of reaction you get by touching your aggressor. Very simply, if your aggressor pulls away sharply from your touch then you know he is highly wound up and ready to go. However, if he lets you maintain contact, then the threat level is lower and he is still in a position to discuss and be reasoned with.

One of my own favourite techniques, particularly in the nightclub environment where you are often physically closer to the aggressor, is to use a Staggered Fence and touch their waist for control (Picture 21).

Picture 21

You are obviously closer to your aggressor so you must be more aware and protected from surprise attack, but touching around the waist is a great way of both passing on your calming energy and also feeling his reaction.

If he reacts in an aggressive way, you will know immediately, as any movement must come through his body (or core) first, and you will sense that.

As soon as you feel this, the basic technique is to sharply and forcefully push the aggressor back and around at the waist, (Pictures 22a and 22b). This throws him off

Picture 22a                     Picture 22b

balance and out of range for his initial attack, but then the fight is on, and you will need to follow up quickly with your support system before he regains his composure and comes back in with an attack of his own.

In summary, the Controlling Fence should:

- enforce a heightened state of awareness;
- have raised hands;
- control distance and personal space;
- be neither aggressive nor submissive;
- monitor the aggressor's movements;
- use calming dialogue;
- prepare you to act; and
- afford you the opportunity to escape.

## Submissive Fence

*Pretend inferiority and encourage his arrogance.*

—Sun Tzu

If you feel the situation has no possible outcome other than physical conflict, then your primary goal should be to hit first and with the maximum effect possible. To do this, you need to give your first punch the best possible chance of it delivering a KO blow.

By feigning submission and acting scared in front of your aggressor, it will have the effect of lowering his adrenalin, and by your actions you are confirming to him that he is bigger, stronger, and more threatening than you are and that you are going to lose this confrontation.

Remember, the reason the aggressor is in front of you in the

first place is because he thinks he can win, and by being submissive you are reaffirming that notion in his own mind. This removes any doubt that he may have had about the outcome of this conflict and in turn allows his adrenalin to subside.

In effect, he begins to celebrate the idea of having already won the fight before it has actually started, and because of this he gets a premature release of endorphin.

No matter how confident he was to begin with, he would still have had some degree of fear and trepidation, which is often the reason for him picking fights in the first place.

Bullies get off on the initial build-up of adrenalin followed by the massive high they get after they are victorious over their lesser victim, so by being submissive (rather, feigning submission), you allow your aggressor that feeling ahead of time.

The important point to remember here is that, in my experience, once you have gone down the submissive route you are almost always destined to end up fighting.

Done well, your actions will have convinced him that you are too scared and weak to put up any kind of resistance to his attack, and, being the bully that he is, he will not think twice about taking advantage of this easy situation and going in for the kill.

I don't think I can recall one incident where playing the submissive card has resulted in the aggressor stopping and saying:

'Oh, you don't want to fight? Oh. OK then. See you!'

It is more often something like:

'Oh, you don't want to fight? Oh. OK then. Have some of this!'

A rain of punches aimed at taking your head off your shoulders and knocking you into the middle of next week swiftly follows.

The technique is to simply go from the Controlling Fence into a Submissive Fence position, by stepping back and raising your hands into a more 'pleading' type of stance. As well as this being a very timid-looking position, it also disguises your move into a small stance and gives you a little extra distance between yourself and the aggressor (Pictures 23a and 23b).

Picture 23a                              Picture 23b

## Creating Distance Using the Submissive Fence

The second important point to remember is that, whilst a Submissive Fence is a great way of getting your aggressor to relax, there is still more that can be done to increase your chances of a successful one-punch KO.

This is to engage your aggressor's brain, or the poor excuse for a brain that they tend to have.

By engaging his brain you take his mind off everything else for a split second: this is your split second of opportunity.

There are several ways to engage the brain, such as pointing at something over their shoulder, interrupting their dialogue with something completely random, but the best method I have found that always works is to ask them a question.

It doesn't matter if this question is logical:

'What did you just say?'

Or illogical:

'Did you know my dog's name was Max?'

Either approach will trip up their thought process of 'I'm going to kick your head around this car park' and force them involuntarily to consider your question, if only for a fleeting moment.

They have to register the question, then process it and decide if it's a sensible question or not. Then they have to decide if the situation is fitting for them to answer it.

The logical question may actually prompt an answer.

The illogical question prompts the same thought process and then an element of confusion over 'what the hell is this guy talking about', and then they have to decide, not what to answer, but whether to answer at all.

Either way, you get a split second, maybe up to half a second of confusion and distraction in your aggressor's mind, and this is the window of opportunity that you have been waiting for and need to take advantage of.

So now when you strike you not only have a physically relaxed opponent, but his brain is also distracted and preoccupied with your question.

Asking a question to engage the brain prior to your attack works very well from a Controlling as well as a Submissive Fence. The submission element merely helps to reinforce the overall message that you are scared and don't want to fight.

We will look at pre-emptive striking later in this manual and also in a future Pre-Emptive Striking Concepts title, but it's worth mentioning now about timing.

A common mistake made is bad timing between asking the question and throwing the initial strike.

Punching too soon is a common mistake, and I see this often in training where the puncher is still mid-question when he throws the first punch, which doesn't give the opponent a chance to register the question, so he will still be switched on when the punch is thrown.

Punching too late is another common mistake and often a result of lack of confidence or simply your own fear, but if we wait too long to deliver the first punch, our aggressor will have processed the question, decided whether it deserves an answer, or concluded that you are nuts and couldn't care less what your dog's name was and readied himself for his onslaught on you.

You are then too late and will have to do some quick thinking to get back in control and try another distracting technique.

As with all these techniques, I have exaggerated the body positions slightly in the accompanying illustrations for the benefits of clearer instruction and explanation, but, in reality, you can be a little more subtle with these positions and obviously not as static as the pictures portray.

From the pictures, you can see how I can use an orthodox stance (left foot forward) with a left-hand lead arm, or a right-hand lead arm (Pictures 24a and 24b).

I can also switch this to put my right foot forward.

Sadly, in a real situation you rarely have the space or time to position your stance subtly into a nice conventional left-leg lead: more often than not you will be square onto your opponent. Any repositioning then will give the game away, so, unfortunately, you are then stuck with the position you are in and will need to control and deliver your initial strikes from this position.

Picture 24a                          Picture 24b

This is why restrictive training is a must in order to develop fast, powerful, explosive punching from any position, lead arm or reverse arm.

You can also see from these pictures that I am deliberately trying to make myself look smaller, almost in a cowering, pleasing way.

Appearing to shrink physically in the face of your aggressor is a great demonstration of what you want him to believe is also happening to your emotional state. Ultimately, you want him to believe the fear is shrinking your strength and your courage.

In summary, the Submissive Fence should:

- only be used when all other avenues have been exhausted;
- be well-acted, feigning fear;
- cause the aggressor to 'switch-off';
- engage the aggressor's brain to create a moment of opportunity;
- increase the chances of an effective pre-emptive strike; and
- allow you to attack until there is no longer a threat, then make your escape.

# Aggressive Fence

*The supreme art of war is to subdue the enemy without fighting.*

—Sun Tzu

The alternative to playing down the situation and feigning submission is to turn the tables and become a monster right before your aggressor's eyes.

This is where you employ the Aggressive Fence, and the intention here is to do the exact opposite of the Submissive Fence.

Your aim is to convince your aggressor that he has just made a big mistake and a huge miscalculation in judging you as potential prey, and not only are you not a suitable prey, but given the chance, you will turn the tables to become predator.

Remember, we are trying to do everything we can to *not* have to fight, and if we can get the aggressor to bottle out and change his mind, then we have succeeded.

The aggressor will already have some adrenalin circling through his body. He will have worked himself up, triggered some adrenal release into his system, and will, most likely, even have some anxiety and a little fear.

What the Aggressive Fence does is add to that fear rather than switch it off as with the Submissive Fence.

We will discuss this more in later chapters, but basically, the aim is to overload our aggressor with fear and uncertainty, trigger adrenal dumps into his system that will push him into fight-or-flight mode, and then we make sure there is sufficient space for him to choose the preferable flight option.

## The Freeze State

If you've ever watched anyone try a bungee jump you will sometimes see them experience the 'freeze state', which is a condition which sits in between fight or flight, or rather, before it.

I also call it the Sticky Feet Syndrome, where you see people standing on the edge of the cage, half wanting to jump and half wanting to climb back into the cage and it looks as though their feet are glued to the edge of the cage, hence 'Sticky Feet'.

This is the period of indecision when they are trying to gain composure and control over the mass of adrenalin coursing through their bodies. Ultimately, what you are doing with the Aggressive Fence is placing the aggressors in this freeze state.

Once they are in freeze state, and whilst they are trying to gather their composure, you need to encourage flight by giving them loopholes and ways out, whilst making the fight option appear a very bad choice by being aggressive.

So from a Controlling Fence you must explode your arms out, making yourself look bigger, and appearing to become enraged and agitated, much like a caged wild animal.

It is most important to use violent, guttural language and be very, very aggressive and demonstrative when you throw those words, insults and threats at your aggressor.

You need to make some space between yourself and the aggressor, and a good way to do this is to use a violent shove/push on your opponent's chest to push him back. Do this at the same time you switch into your aggressive mode (Pictures 25a, 25b, and 25c).

As with being submissive, this is all about acting, and even if you don't think you can act, if someone says your life is on the line, if you don't pretend to be a certain type of person, I'm positive you will soon start playing the lead role very convincingly and very quickly.

Picture 25a

Picture 25b

Picture 25c

The Aggressive Fence is particularly good against multiple attackers, or when you really don't want to fight this person, and is the option I choose more frequently than the Submissive Fence.

I've said already that the last thing I want to do is fight. So, assuming I wasn't able to defuse the situation at a Controlling Fence stage, all things being equal, given the choice I will choose the Aggressive Fence every time. Go submissive and you will almost certainly be fighting, but go aggressive and you're more likely to avoid physical conflict altogether.

However, in addition, I will also choose the Aggressive Fence if the guy in front of me looks particularly capable, particularly violent, out of my league, a known gangster that I really don't want in my life, or backed up by a group of other guys who may all want to join in when it kicks off.

The Aggressive Fence also buys me more time. It adds a few extra seconds into the dialogue phase of the confrontation and gives me the opportunity to send messages and signals to all of the aggressor's friends as well as himself.

## Ballooning and Posturing

Ballooning and Posturing (Pictures 26a and 26b) are just some descriptions of techniques which are an addition and supplement to the Aggressive Fence.

Picture 26a                                    Picture 26b

These bolstering techniques are particularly useful when you are faced with more than one aggressor or potential attacker and simply reinforce the 'monster' message you are trying to deliver.

The simplest way to describe this is for you to watch any footage of real street fights, but pay particular attention to the body language during the pre-fight build-up.

You will see the aggressor(s) pacing, pointing, gesturing, neck-pecking (turkey style), thrusting hands and arms out, sticking their chests out, their chins out, wide-eyed, sucking in their bottom lip, even foaming at the mouth, and so for you to employ effective ballooning and posturing techniques you need to reproduce this as accurately as possible.

Remember, you are simply acting the part, so play this part well: you may not win an Oscar, but you may just get home in one piece. I've never been one for awards and trophies anyway; some may say that's a good job because I was never good enough to win any.

Ballooning is best applied directly after the explosive shove that you use when switching to the Aggressive Fence. Backing this movement up immediately with big gestures, aggressive and arrogant body language, lots of pointing and directing your threats, particularly if you are faced with numbers.

This may seem like a very risky tack to take, but your only other option is to go submissive and know that you are definitely going to have to fight.

It's entirely your decision to make as to whether you think you are going to have to throw the first punch, or if you feel that you have a chance in psyching your aggressor(s) out with an aggressive approach.

But always bear in mind that you may still have to back this up, so be prepared and be ready with your first shot.

I have implemented this extremely successfully on many occasions, but as always, there have been exceptions.

On one occasion, I went aggressive and it just didn't wash with the guy, a hardened fighter who was quite happy to take it to whatever level I wanted to go to, much to my dismay.

This is where I really took a liberty and got away with it, because instead of going aggressive, it failing, and going straight into physical, I turned it back around and went for a subtly submissive stance instead.

I exploded with a shove to gain some space, and followed with

ballooning, and throwing guttural verbal threats at him.
He responded with equal aggression and started to move back towards me.
Ordinarily, I would have used this movement as my trigger to throw my first punch but it just didn't feel right. My distance was off, which left me slightly out of range and with this guy now playing aggression poker. 'I'll see your explosive shove and Aggressive Fence and I will now raise you with another verbal insult and a threatening move forwards.'
So, instead, I switched to a Submissive Fence. I knew if I went too submissive he would see straight through it. I mean, one minute I'm exploding into his face and the next I'm playing the timid little cat routine.
So I chose to take a small step back and act as though I had just realised I'd made a big mistake.
'Look, I'm sorry. Let's just talk about this.'
The switch from aggressive to partially submissive was enough to throw the aggressor for a second – which gave me my window to throw my best shot.
I actually knocked this guy out for quite some time, which was probably due to the step forward that I had to take to recover the distance I had created with the Aggressive Fence, so nothing in this life is guaranteed, and choosing an Aggressive Fence with lots of ballooning is no exception.
Here are some things to keep in mind if, at first, it doesn't work.

## Keep Going

If you go aggressive with lots of ballooning and it doesn't appear to be working, keep going. Don't give in too soon.
Keep turning on the pressure. So long as they aren't stepping forward to recover the space you've created with the explosive shove, then you're doing it right. It means they are now registering your actions and trying to work it out and are now busy dealing with the internal turmoil that you have triggered. Confusion like this can often leave the aggressor a little dumbstruck for a few seconds, so you may not see any outward reactions in either an aggressive or submissive way immediately.

If you're trying to psych out a group with ballooning and posturing, and it doesn't seem to be working, then you can try some of the following.

## Isolation

I call this technique 'isolation', because this is what you are trying to do when you have a group of individuals and you want to direct some aggression at them singularly rather than en masse.

I've often found that in a group of aggressors there will be only a small percentage who really want to fight; the majority will either only get involved when it looks like it's going their way, or won't want to get involved at all, but equally don't want to be seen as cowards amongst their peers.

Direct some aggression at individuals in the group: try to scare off one or two individuals in the group with direct threats, precise, projected aggression with pointing.

This will at least help even up the numbers a little, but I don't mean that I expect these individuals to go running off leaving their friends behind. They will still stay where they are, but you will have scared the fight out of them, so that they are less likely to get involved should the whole thing blow up.

### Even Up the Odds

Try reducing the numbers of the group by directly challenging the main aggressor, or ringleader.

### Direct Challenge

Offer a square go – and match fight or one-on-one.

Often, this will give the friends a way out, particularly those who are now starting to doubt whether this was the best thing they could be doing with their spare time on a Saturday night out anyway.

### Loophole

Always leave an opening for the aggressor to escape – give him a way out.

Don't corner him otherwise you may not leave him any option but to attack, and even when you have beaten him, let him save face.

They are more likely to leave without fighting if they can save a little face, even when they have just bottled it due to your extreme aggression.

## Assign Jobs

This works particularly well when you have one main attacker with a group of friends.

Once you've exploded and postured in front of them, give his friends some jobs to do. Tell them to take their friend, the lead antagonist, away before he gets battered.

This serves a few purposes. It gives them a job to do which inadvertently tells them they are now no longer in the fight. They should be happy to adopt this role.

It gives the lead attacker a way out, because he can now wait for his friends to take him away.

It allows the lead attacker to save some face as he can shout lots of insults on how, if it wasn't for his friends, he would have made your head into a canoe, or something equally creative.

The ballooning and Aggressive Fence is the same as your one-punch KO. It doesn't always work.

And just as your support system should kick-in when your first punch doesn't do the business, so your support system needs to kick-in if your ballooning fails.

## Escape

What if it does work? How do you move away after ballooning without appearing to be running off?

First, there's nothing wrong with running away, so if your posturing and ballooning gives you extra distance, extra time, puts an element of hesitation in your aggressors, then it's fine to run away: you've done your job.

However, again, if the ballooning is successful, you should have left your aggressors in a state of having lost. They should be beaten men. Do it well enough and they will be hoping you walk away sooner than later – they will be praying you go without backing up what you've just threatened them with.

So either you can walk away, or you can give them the opening to do so.

Beat them with aggression and then tell them to feck off.

If that doesn't work, direct your threats at one of the group, then tell his mates to take him away.

They will be over the moon that they are no longer in the fight and their only role now is to drag their friend away.

Their friend will also be more than happy that he can let his friends drag him away, and even save a bit of face by throwing a few verbal threats back in your direction as he goes.

How many times have you seen lads get dragged off by their girlfriends? If they wanted to fight for real, no girlfriend would be able to stop them getting to you (unless she's my sister, of course, but she's an exception), so it's clear they don't really want to fight and their girlfriend provides the perfect way for them to escape without losing face.

An important point to note is that there is a fine line between using effective posturing and inadvertently inflaming the situation and inviting the fight to escalate.

It's important to get your body language right. A mistake such as the one shown in Pictures 27a and 27b, where the posturing is

Picture 27a

Picture 27b

calling in the aggressor, leaves them no option. He has to save face, and the only way he can do that is move forward to fight, which is not what you want, and you must be careful that your posturing is merely to make yourself look stronger, more aggressive, and more ferocious. It is not to challenge the aggressor, as this eliminates any loopholes and exits you may have previously given him.

In summary, the Aggressive Fence should:
- be your preferred option if you want to avoid fighting;
- include posturing and ballooning;
- push the aggressor into a freeze state;
- encourage flight in your aggressor rather than fight;
- be used when faced with multiple attackers;
- include all the tricks – aggressor isolation, loopholing, assigning jobs, direct threats; and
- afford you the opportunity to escape.

# Playing the Situation Down

### Why Play the Situation Down?

Every situation is different, so your actions and decisions will be a result of the external factors present at the time, e.g., your location and surroundings, your options for escape, the number of aggressors you are faced with, the quantum of potential back-up and support you have, the presence of others in your company who will also require protection, the presence of weapons, etc.

Playing the situation down means to try to use calming, inoffensive body language and dialogue to defuse the situation and calm things down for all parties involved.

### Using a Controlling Fence

Using a Controlling Fence whilst pacifying the situation can have good results, but the important thing is to remain assertive and confident. Once you move into a Controlling Fence position, your attacker will often get a subconscious feeling that it's not wise for him to proceed with his planned course of action.

Whilst consciously they will not see anything untoward, subconsciously they will be picking up on your confidence, your body language, your choice of words and your assertive authority.

Clever use of language can literally interrupt the aggressors' attack rituals and cause them to think again.

This was something I had great success with when working on the nightclub doors, and while the added authority of being the doorman obviously helped when instructing people to behave in certain ways, it still had to be enforced correctly.

Being assertive with a Controlling Fence was absolutely the best solution, as it meant the aggressor was pacified and prevented from causing trouble, no punches were thrown, and there were no big scenes of aggressive ballooning and posturing on the part of the door team.

## Using a Submissive Fence

If you opt to really play the situation down with a Submissive Fence, the results can be very much different.

There is a big difference between managing a Controlling Fence with dialogue that *instructs* the aggressor to calm down, and a Submissive Fence that *pleads* with the aggressor to calm down.

Both are valid techniques but have a very different result and their own particular place in the self-protection process.

As we've already discussed, if someone is in front of you and is making plans to mug, fight with, attack, or control you in some way, feigning submission only reaffirms to the aggressor that you are a suitable victim.

Aggressors are simply bullies looking for soft targets and will almost always mistake your softness and reluctance to fight back as a sign of weakness, which is exactly what they are looking for.

In my years of experience, I don't think that I can recall one instance where I have played down a potentially violent confrontation with a Submissive Fence and not had to back this up with physical intervention on my part.

Because of this, as I've already discussed earlier in this manual, playing down a situation and going submissive must be seen as your introduction to your pre-emptive strike.

## Under what Circumstances would You Use this Tactic?

I will emphasise again that physical conflict should be the last thing we choose and our last port of call.

Once a situation moves into physical conflict you will be in that world until it is over, and no matter how good you are, there are no guarantees.

I would only try to play a situation down based on the following two rules.

1. If I have a very strong gut feeling that using calming dialogue and reasoning with the attacker will actually dissuade him from continuing with his attack and threatening behaviour.

    If this is the case, I always maintain a Controlling Fence whilst trying to calm things down.

    I do this with a confident and self-assured approach and use language such as:

    'Let's all just calm down.'

    'There's no need to be like that.'

    'Chill out - just hang on a minute.'

    These are all instructions that I am *telling* the attacker to calm down, rather than *pleading* with him to calm down.

2. If I feel that I have no other options left open to me and that the only way to end this situation is to throw the first punch and try to get the guy out of the game as quickly as possible.

If I have no way to escape safely, if I know that I am only seconds away from being physically attacked, and if I am truly in a life-threatening situation, then I will opt for a Submissive Fence position and then use dialogue such as:
'Please, can't we just talk about it?'
'I don't want to fight.'
'Will you please calm down?'

This kind of dialogue reaffirms the actions and body language of a Submissive Fence, but be prepared: it will almost certainly prompt the attacker to move forward and step up the attack into a more physical mode.

## What Will be the Results?

From a Controlling Fence using calming instructions, it's possible the attacker will think again, but you need to be clever with this and always provide the aggressor with ways out, so that he can halt his attack while still maintaining 'face'.

From a Submissive Fence with pleading dialogue and distracting questions, the result will most definitely be the aggressor moving forward to take the attack to the next level.

This is your window of opportunity to attack with your pre-emptive strike and to end the fight in one shot, or as quickly as possible.

I don't think I can recall one single instance where, after I've pleaded with an aggressor, 'Please, can't we just talk about it?' the aggressor has responded with, 'Oh – OK then!'

It just never happens – so be prepared.

# Playing the Situation Up

### Why Play the Situation Up?

Wherever the situation allows, I like to play the situation up.

And whilst this may seem like an aggressive action on my part, it's the best way to avoid the situation escalating into physical conflict.

By choosing to step up into an Aggressive Fence, with the addition of ballooning and posturing, you are trying to convince the aggressor that he has made a mistake and chosen the wrong target.

I prefer this option for several reasons.

The first is that, in my experience, it is the best way to avoid having to fight.

It means that you can end the situation without having to throw any punches and becoming physical, and it also means that the aggressor can leave the situation unharmed.

When faced with multiple assailants or weapons, not fighting is always the preferred option.

The only alternative is to get your first shot in to try to even up the odds a little, and that would mean reverting to a Submissive

Fence, but it's still valid; it's for you to decide.

It sows an element of doubt, not only in your attacker, but in those looking on.

I've seen on many occasions people thinking they are only facing one person, only to have cowardly individuals step out from the crowd when the fight has kicked off, throw a few cheeky kicks or punches of their own, then fade back into the onlooking crowd again.

Extremely cowardly types, often these are people who don't even know those who are fighting. However, it happens, and becoming aggressive may just make such individuals think twice as well.

That is also a good reason not to become too target-focused, which we look at in the Mistakes chapter.

## Under what Circumstances would You Use this Tactic?

As has already been said, the situation has to be right for this to work.

Sometimes you will have no option but to throw the first punch: being aggressive may do nothing other than escalate the situation.

But even then, once the deception has been used and the first punch thrown, you should immediately become aggressive and demonstrative, particularly if the fight is not over and you are still under threat.

So the time to become aggressive is when you really feel like you cannot win the physical conflict.

If you are outnumbered, if you sense that they are not 100 per cent committed to the situation themselves, or if you are facing weapons.

I used the Aggressive Fence particularly well against a guy who became hostile towards me with a knuckleduster.

As this was only one attacker, and I had been switched on enough to see this situation about two or three seconds in advance of the initial assault, I could have opted for a Controlling, then a

Submissive Fence, and then gone in with my pre-emptive strike and hopefully knocked him out.

That would have been a valid solution as I was not able to make my escape at the time.

However, I opted for an Aggressive Fence, which worked exceptionally well.

This guy had not expected me to become equally aggressive back at him, and the fact that he had a weapon told me he was under-confident, and was clearly expecting me to back off under the potential danger of this.

On this occasion, instead of using an aggressive shove, I delivered a Thai leg kick to his thigh/knee area, which shocked him and added to his own adrenalin. It also gave me some extra space to throw more threats at him, and the result was he started to back off, with all the usual threats of coming back to get me next week, etc.

## What Will be the Results?

If you play the aggressive monster act well, the result will be a massive adrenal overload in your aggressor(s), which will put them in a state of freeze, from which you should encourage them to leave instead of fight.

This is done by both making the fight option a not-very-pleasant prospect by continuing to balloon and posture, and by giving them ways of implementing their flight mechanism with loopholes and verbal exits.

Do this well and the situation will be over, or at least delayed sufficiently for you to make your own escape, and, if nothing else, the aggressive shove or kick that creates a gap between you and your assailants could be enough for you to turn and run.

# Attacks From the Fence

As it has already been said, in a self-protection scenario, escape must always be our first option.

We should be practising effective awareness, assessment, and avoidance tactics that will hopefully allow us to avoid any life-threatening conflict.

When this has failed us, or circumstances have resulted in our not being able to escape, our next most important tool is to use effective attacks that will bring the conflict to an end as quickly as possible, with the least possible danger or injury to ourselves.

Knowing when to attack is very difficult, and ultimately you will need to rely on your own instinct and intuition to help guide you as to when the situation has escalated to a point of no return.

However, attacking first is extremely difficult, and there are lots of emotional barriers that can get in the way and prevent us from being able to strike pre-emptively. I will discuss these in a later chapter, so for now, we will assume that you have mastered these emotions and are now looking to mount an effective attack.

Your attacks may differ depending on which Fence position you are deploying them from, so I will take each position in turn.

The following techniques are all that either I or others I know and respect and have used in real-life situations, whether in professional security roles or in real-life personal assaults.

## Go for a KO: Strikes

The one thing I will say is that the majority, if not all, of the attacks in this chapter are primarily focused on knocking out the aggressor rather than simply hurting or distracting him, such as

in Picture 28 where I am aiming
a left hook to the jaw.

In my experience, the only
time I will slap, punch, kick, or
shove someone with the
intention of only shocking them
or administering pain is during
part of the Aggressive Fence
process, where I want to force
an adrenal dump on the
attacker and use some kind of
shock factor.

Picture 28

Once the adrenalin is flowing in an assailant, or particularly if
he is under the influence of drugs, pain becomes less effective
in terminating a threat.

I have personally had teeth smashed, ribs broken, fingers and
hands broken during fights and not only has it not stopped my
progress, I often didn't even feel it until after the fight was
over.

This is the effect of adrenalin, which we will look at later, not
because I am some superhuman being (well, maybe I am a little).

I've also delivered massive leg kicks, blows that have broken
noses, jaws, even arms while grappling individuals, and it has
not stopped them either.

So, for me, my primary aim with any attack I deliver from the
Fence is to render the assailant unconscious, and I do this by
knocking him out, either with blows to the jaw, which shake the
brain and cause it to shut down, or with chokes and strangles
which cut off air supply and oxygen to the brain temporarily.

Without going into great detail, the main reason for hitting
the jaw is to create a shaking of the brain. The jawline acts as a
lever which jolts the skull, causing the brain to whiplash, the
trauma from which will cause it to shut down in self-preservation.

Consequently, the greater the shaking of the brain you can
generate, the more chances of a KO and also the longer the
duration of unconsciousness.

Accuracy is vital, particularly as your target moves further down
the jawline to the point of the jaw. Here, you will get a bigger
KO, but it's a much smaller target to hit.

*The Smaller the Target, the Bigger the Prize.*

It's not enough to be a heavy hitter. You must be sharp, explosive, and accurate. I have friends of 8 and 9 stone who are prolific KO merchants because they are fast, explosive, and accurate. So don't be fooled into thinking you cannot knock someone out because you are small or light or because he's much bigger and stronger than you.

Likewise, don't be fooled into thinking that because you can hit the punch bag so hard it winces that you are going to be able to knock people out easily. Once adrenalin is flowing and your target has reduced considerably in size, you may not have as much success as you think.

The final point in gaining the best KO with a strike is to use deception and have a relaxed recipient rather than one who knows what's coming. If you give any signs of your intention to throw an attack, they will instinctively react by tensing and recoiling, which means that not only are you likely to miss the target, you will have more difficulty in creating the whiplash effect on the head and brain that you need.

Deception is key, which is why feigning submission and engaging the brain are pivotal factors in delivering effective pre-emptive strikes from the Fence.

## Go for a KO: Chokes/Strangles

KOs with chokes and strangles occur by the nature of cutting off the oxygen supply to the brain, an example of which can be seen in Picture 29.

A choke closes down the windpipe with your forearm or wrist or any other mechanism, which prevents air from entering the lungs.

This will usually result in a panic, gag reaction from your assailant, and something you must be careful of as you can often lose your grip due to this sudden explosion in panic strength from your recipient.

Picture 29

With a strangle, the intention is to close down the carotid arteries which run to the brain up the side of the neck. This cuts off oxygen (carried by the blood) to the brain and can sometimes go undetected by the recipient until it is too late and he's unconscious.

This is my favoured technique as it is usually a much tighter hold to have, and causes less panic reaction from the recipient. It also works a bit faster.

The longer you hold these techniques on, the longer your assailant will remain unconscious. So please be careful, because if you hold these grips on for too long they go to sleep forever, or at least wake up with brain damage.

All this stuff is deadly and must not be used carelessly or without control.

## Attacks

The following are some examples of attacks that can be delivered from each of the Fence positions discussed.

It's not my intention to tell you which attack to use, which is your personal choice and you will need to select attacks that will fit your body type, suit the styles you may have already trained in, and the situation at the time.

All I will say is to make any attack you throw explosive and violently aggressive, with total intent on taking the other person out of the game.

You get one shot, so make it count, and if that doesn't work, you are most likely fighting for real, which is where all your support system, your boxing, karate, grappling training comes in.

The only difference when punching from the various Fence positions will be things such as distancing, and range of movement.

For example, when punching from a Submissive Fence, your hands will be raised and probably very close to the intended target, which means you will have very little time to wind up the attack.

This is where restrictive punching and restrictive training comes in, which will be covered in a separate instruction manual.

## Deception

To begin with, we will look at the deception tactics you can use to help disguise your attack.

*Being Tactile.* Test the waters by touching an arm, which can quickly be turned into a hold where you clasp around the back of the arm, just above the elbow and spin the aggressor. This is useful for manhandling individuals, but not exactly a finishing move on its own (Pictures 30a, 30b, and 30c).

Picture 30b

Picture 30a

*Feigning Hardness of Hearing.* This is a good way to get closer to your target, and also move your head out of the line of fire, without it appearing too obvious.

Picture 30c

I couple this with a question such as, 'What did you say?' and is particularly useful in noisy bars and clubs. It also doubles up beautifully with a slap or punch as it allows a massive winding-up of the technique, and can even bring the attack in behind the aggressor's peripheral vision, as shown in Pictures 31a and 31b.

Picture 31a                                          Picture 31b

This can work on either side, left or right.

It is the question that creates the moment of opportunity to deliver the first shot. It also allows you to disguise your build-up to the shot by giving you a reason to be moving into such a position. The open hands are indicative of questioning and not aggression, but have moved into a position that gives great range of motion before the attack lands on its target.

## Lead Hand Attacks

*Hook*. A great punch, even though it's off the lead leg (so gets less power from the hips), is effective due to the speed, accuracy and ability to be delivered undetected, outside the recipient's field of vision.

Hand positions and direction of attack can vary depending on the situation and your personal preference, as can be seen in Pictures 32a, 32b, and 32c.

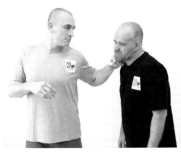

Picture 32a

Picture 32b

Picture 32c

*Uppercut.* I've worked this mostly as a follow-up shot to my first pre-emptive strike, when that hasn't completely done the job. I know: hard to believe, but it has happened. (I do hope you understand the humour in that last joke, otherwise you're going to think I'm some big-headed wannabe.)

Be careful with this strike as it can catch the body on the way up to the chin, which is not ideal.

*Slap.* One of my favourite techniques and one that I've had a great deal of

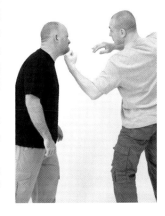

success with. The slap allows you to keep your hand relaxed even at the point of delivery and contact. The more relaxed you are with your techniques, the more powerful and explosive they will be, so a slap is perfect for helping you to stay relaxed during the delivery.

I particularly like using the slap from a Submissive Fence as your hand is already very close to the target and requires very little adjustment from its submissive, pleading position, to the contact with the side of the jaw.

KOs from the slap are also a result of shaking the brain, although there are schools of thought which suggest the resulting pain spread over a wide area of the face is enough to cause the brain to shut down. In addition, some will deliver the slap cupped across the ear to damage eardrums and upset balance, possibly causing a KO too.

*Elbow*. These are devastating attacks, but require you to be much closer to your target. Stepping in with these attacks can

sometimes give the game away, so it's better if you are already close before launching the attack.

There are many ways to throw elbows: diagonally up, down, horizontal. Whatever you choose, ensure you maintain accurate targeting and drive through the target with the point of your elbow.

## Reverse Hand Attacks

*Cross.* The right cross is a classic attack from the Fence and one which I drill relentlessly from a variety of positions and stances. You will notice in Picture 33 that my left hand is also high in these pictures: this is because I'm throwing the punch from a Submissive Fence, which creates

Picture 33

restriction and limited movement in the build-up to the punch.

You will also notice that I vary the angle of the cross so that sometimes it merges into a right hook rather than a straight right cross (Pictures 34a and 34b). The reason I do this is to help

Picture 34a                                          Picture 34b

ensure I make contact with the jawline target. Aiming directly straight onto the point of the chin is actually quite a small target to hit, and easily missed in the heat of the moment. A fraction of an inch either to the left or right and you will skim past the front of the jaw and slide up the side, probably negating the KO. By turning the punch slightly into a hook, you will hit the side of the jaw, which affords you more room for targeting error.

While I've never thrown a left jab (lead arm punch) from the Fence position, I have thrown a left cross, i.e. from a reverse hand position with my right foot forward.

This was a result of positioning at the time of the attack and not being able to change footwork without it being noticed by the assailant. Because of this, I like to train techniques from all angles and stances, with both hands, while still concentrating a large proportion of my training on my favourite two or three techniques.

*Hook.* This is probably one of my favourite attacks from the Fence, and one that I have had the most success with.

Picture 35 may not depict a conventional or aesthetically clas-sic right hook, but that is not the intention. This particu-lar hook has been thrown from a Controlling Fence where the distance was de-liberately close. Conse-quently, the punch has to be adapted to suit the close-ness of the range and most direct angle between the starting position of the hand and the jawline target.

Picture 35

Varying distance and punching angles is a must when training in these techniques in order to find the most efficient and effective strikes for you.

As with the left hook, some different angles of attack for the right hook can include a slightly upward motion, horizontally, or even in a downward chopping motion. All are valid, try them (Pictures 36a, 36b, and 36c).

*Uppercut.* This is another devastating punch, but requires lots of practice in order to achieve: first, the confidence to throw it; and second, the accuracy without glancing off arms or the chest

Picture 36a

Picture 36b

Picture 36c

on the way up to the jawline target. This is particularly good from very close range and is also very well hidden by being below the peripheral field of vision of the aggressor.

Notice also the variation in the hand position in Pictures 37a and 37b. From a Submissive Fence with hands raised high, there is very little distance and time in which to turn the hand into the conventional 'palm facing inwards' position. Consequently, I work a lot on punching without twisting the hand from the start to finish position. The result is an uppercut with the palm facing sideways.

Picture 37a

Picture 37b

Regardless of hand position, the important point is to ensure you always hit the jaw with your two main knuckles.

*Slap.* As with the lead hand slap, this is a great technique due to its natural action. We all instinctively know how to slap, which means that not only will it be easier to condition as a natural response, but it is also more likely to hit the target.

*Elbow.* As with the lead hand elbow, distancing is crucial with elbow attacks, and this is something that must be drilled in order to develop your own sense of distancing and range.

*Head Butts.* These are most effective when in very close, but I have seen others work them from quite long range by launching themselves into their target. I've found them to work best when coupled with a Controlling Fence where you first adjust your position under the guise of feigning

hardness of hearing or asking a question, as shown in Picture 38. This allows you to create an element of hip wind-up in preparation for firing your head into the target.

The general rule of thumb is to ensure you hit with any part of your head above your own eyeline (forehead), to any part of the recipient's head below his eyeline (jaw, nose, face).

Picture 38

My preference is to lower my own body before I drive forward with the attack, rather than try to head-butt in a downward direction to hit the jaw, as can be seen in Pictures 39, 40a, 40b, and 40c. But this is my preference and not for everyone.

Picture 39

Picture 40a          Picture 40b          Picture 40c

*Choke or Strangle.* The preferred technique I have used on many occasions has been a rear strangle. You need to be positioned either to the side, or, ideally, behind your attacker, and the best way to do this is to spin him, and yourself, by first attacking his upper body/shoulders. From a Fence position, push the right shoulder away from you and simultaneously pull his left shoulder towards you. Do this explosively and you should get him to turn counterclockwise. However, even if he doesn't turn at all (perhaps he's particularly large or heavy), you use his body to spin yourself around him, trying to get as far around behind him as possible. Then allow your right hand to move up to the neck/throat position and tie up your hand using your left arm, as shown in Pictures 41a, 41b, 41c, and 41d.

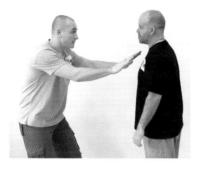

Picture 41a

Picture 41b

Picture 41c

Picture 41d

These techniques, although appearing very simple, have a lot of intricate details that can all help to make them more efficient, less vulnerable to escape and faster to generate the KO. We will look at this in more detail in another instruction manual.

Whilst it may not be as fast-acting or as 'tight' a technique, it

Picture 42

is possible to get the choke/ strangle from the side of your attacker if you fail to get completely around to his back (Picture 42).

## Attacks Leading to the Aggressive Fence and Ballooning

All the previous attacks are intended to render your attacker unconscious rather than simply hurt or stun him.

However, if you intend to move into an Aggressive Fence position coupled with ballooning and posturing, the best way to do this is with some kind of shock, adrenalin-inducing attack.

We have already seen the aggressive shove in an earlier chapter and this would be my preferred choice of attack because it serves several purposes.

It gives a sudden rush of adrenalin to the aggressor, it pushes him backwards, and also allows you to step back, gaining some safe space, and it may give you sufficient space to immediately escape, or possibly even push him over.

Another attack that I have used successfully is the low Thai or roundhouse kick, aimed either at the aggressor's knee, outer thigh, or inner thigh (Pictures 43a and 43b).

I've used this when I have been faced with an attacker who was 'tooled-up' and it caused sufficient pain and shock to cause him to back off.

It's simply a low roundhouse kick, delivered off either your lead or rear leg, but the important thing is to retract once you

Picture 43a                              Picture 43b

have delivered the kick rather than stepping in. We are still trying to create space with this attack, so be careful not to follow through and end up clashing with the aggressor (unless, of course, you wish to use this as a lead attack followed by a flurry of punches perhaps).

As I have already said, do not expect this type of attack to stop the fight: it's main aim is to use the shock element that dumps adrenalin into your aggressor. Unless you absolutely destroy your attacker's knee so that he involuntarily falls down, you are not likely to stop him through pain alone.

As with all these techniques, find your own way. Find what techniques suit you best, then drill them until you are sick of them. That is the only way to make these techniques instinctive and effective in high-stress, confrontational situations.

Don't over-complicate the techniques, keep them simple and work them with restrictions that limit your build-up movement so that you can throw them from any angle and from any Fence position.

Above all, they must be explosive and delivered with ferocious intent. Accuracy, speed and intent are far more important than power.

# Common Mistakes

Not every result from a pre-emptive strike is a KO. So it's worth mentioning some of the common mistakes that we make when using the Fence and delivering pre-emptive strikes that lead us to undesirable results.

- *Holding the Fence in an unnatural position for too long.*
  This is partly a result of this subject being taught and learned through books of this type, and a reason I have produced an accompanying DVD. We get what we train for, so if we train the Fence in a static manner without being fluid or natural with our arm positions and movement, this is what we will get when we do it for real.

Picture 44a

Picture 44b

Picture 44c

A static Fence is easily bypassed by an attacker, even one who loves the camera and an admiring public (Pictures 44a, 44b, and 44c).

- *Appearing aggressive or submissive when actually trying to simply calm the situation and appear passive.*
  Using incorrect body language will give a confusing impression to the aggressor, so when trying to simply calm the situation down, be careful not to be too forceful and aggressive, nor too submissive. The same goes for any other Fence position. Practise using the correct body language and actions for the Fence position required.
- *Making contact with the aggressor: prodding or poking.*
  When trying to control space, make sure you do this with open hands in an assertive way. The moment you start poking and prodding your aggressor, you will only anger him more and possibly escalate a situation that you could have talked down.
- *Using incorrect/inappropriate language: verbal and physical body language.*
  Make sure your dialogue and voice match your actions. So if you are going aggressive, saying things like, 'Stay back, you rotten scoundrel' will most likely not work!
  Guttural, aggressive language, as 'Fecking stay there or I'll rip your fecking head off' will help show you are of an animalistic level and support your body language.
  Feel free to replace fecking with any other appropriate word: I've only used that as my mum may read this book and I don't want her to ban me from her Sunday dinners.
- *Telegraphing the attack.*
  A reason for restrictive training is to learn to strike with minimal build-up or wind-up to your punch. If you have to retract your arm in order to wind up or cock your hips in order to deliver a powerful shot, this can be spotted by your aggressor, unless, of course, you find a way of disguising this movement by dialogue or other actions.
  Things like dropping your left hand before throwing your punch, or reaching out wide to your right before throwing your right hook should be avoided at all costs as they can

Picture 45a                              Picture 45b

give your aggressor advance
warning or the time to prepare
for the shot or even attack first,
as can be seen in Pictures 45a,
45b, and 45c.

- *Misreading the situation.*
  Remember: we train in order to
  be more confident and more
  self-controlled,  balanced
  individuals. It's important that
  we don't enter this world of
  constant  paranoia  and
  aggressive posturing in the hope

Picture 45c

that this will fend off would-be attackers. It may, but at the
same time it will also scare away potential friends and a lot of
good things that may have otherwise entered our lives.

If you live in a state of constant worry and fear of violent
attack, you are quite likely to draw that into your world.

So, when someone next approaches you in the street and is
actually only asking for directions, do this with caution but

try not to immediately launch into an aggressive shove followed by a tirade of verbal abuse. He may only have been lost!

- *Tunnel vision; adrenalin effects; focusing on one target, etc.*
  The effects of adrenalin are many, and unless we are familiar with these side effects, a lot of them will have a detrimental effect on how we operate under the stress of a violent encounter.

  Tunnel vision will cause us to be target-focused, which, although helping us monitor in great detail what our primary aggressor is doing, also prevents us from seeing other potential attackers who may be approaching from another angle.

- *Waiting too long.*
  Attacking first with a pre-emptive strike is a lot easier said than done. (Although I've found it to be fairly difficult to write about, to be honest – you've probably guessed if you've managed to read this far!)

  Our fears can cause us to hesitate and delay throwing our first attack, which could be all the aggressor needs to mount

his own attack. Remember, we are throwing our own pre-emptive attack because we feel we have no other option and are in imminent danger. Hesitate for too long, and that danger will become reality, with your aggressor rearranging your face for you.

- *Not exhausting all options before attacking.*
  The opposite of waiting too long may be to attack too soon. Not exhausting all other options can land you in serious trouble with the law, and even if not, may mean you have attacked someone when you didn't really need to. Whilst we all make mistakes, ultimately that can be seen as bullying and not what we are here for.

- *Lack of commitment in the chosen technique or course of action.*

  Once you have decided to launch a pre-emptive attack, you must commit yourself to it fully. Fear can cause you to pull your punch or subconsciously try to keep your body away from your aggressor while you strike him. Lack of commitment will result in lack of power and accuracy in your attack, potentially reducing your chances of a KO.

- *Missing the target.*
  Missing the target is a common mistake, one that I have done myself on several occasions, sometimes missing the specific target area, such as the jaw, and hitting the teeth, nose, or cheek instead. I've even been known to miss completely, much to the amusement of my fellow doormen and stunned confusion of the intended recipient (re-enacted here in Pictures 46a, 46b, and 46c).

Picture 46a                                    Picture 46b

There are lots of reasons for this, such as being too anxious to get the fight over with, or not focusing on the target correctly.

Picture 46c

- *Bad timing between a distracting question and a pre-emptive strike.*
  This is a common mistake I see when people are training the Fence and that is to not leave a sufficient pause between asking the brain-engaging question and launching your pre-emptive strike.
  You need to give the aggressor time to register your question, somewhere up to half a second. If you ask a question and then immediately throw your attack, the question will not have had time to register and will have been wasted, resulting in the aggressor still being alert to your physical actions and his own game plan.
- *We all make mistakes.*
  Everyone makes mistakes, even me. Yes, that's right, even me: hard to believe, I know.
  Sometimes things don't work out the way you had planned or predicted.
  The ability to adapt when these things happen is the key to survival, and, while the concepts outlined in this manual will go a long way to helping you avoid and survive violent confrontations, a solid, effective support system from any of the variety of martial arts is still essential.

# Action Triggers

One of the biggest problems is knowing when to attack, and then making yourself actually take the step to initiate the attack.

When the time is right and you're left with no other option, taking charge and throwing the first punch can be the toughest part of the proceedings.

One technique I and a lot of my contemporaries utilise is a concept called Action Triggers, or Anchors, as NLP might put it.

I'm no NLP guru, but I have found that if I link my physical action to a sound or a natural movement on my part, I can then remove my conscious thoughts from the process and throw my pre-emptive strike instinctively.

The best action trigger to use is the standard questioning statement you make that is designed to engage the brain of your aggressor (assuming he has one), and distracting him momentarily before you throw your punch or slap.

When you train in these techniques, always include the distracting question as part of your drill: this will help to enforce the trigger element so that your body becomes used to recognising that when it hears you say a particular phrase or word; it knows the next action is to strike.

Don't worry, this doesn't mean if you hear someone say your keyword or phrase you're going to flip into 'Kill All' mode, but it will help remove that slight pause or hesitation in throwing the first punch.

The other important factor with an action trigger is that it helps set your mind to ready for the attack. If you add realism to your training, and if you train with lots of emotive aggression and animalistic intent when you strike, this will all become linked to your action trigger.

Now when you are in a Controlling or Submissive Fence position and ask your brain-engaging question, not only will it help you to progress and throw the first punch, it will also activate the mindset you had in training, which was of extreme venom and aggression.

This is due to the fact that, once the first punch has been thrown, if it hasn't had the desired effect of knocking the guy out, you will need to follow this up with more attacks until he is no longer a threat. It is at this point that the fight is on and there is no more need to feign submission: you now need to be a ferocious monster who will not stop until the threat is over. It is your mindset, not your techniques that will achieve this for you.

# What is Fear? The Effects of Adrenalin

We all feel fear, particularly in uncomfortable situations, alien environments, potentially dangerous and life-threatening confrontations.

Fear is how we internally translate the chemical cocktails that course through our bodies in high-stress situations, and because it is a feeling, an emotion, rather than a physical effect, we are able to reprogramme and desensitise ourselves to these feelings with time and practice.

Fight-or-flight is now a common phrase for the description of the process that occurs instinctively in our bodies in dangerous situations. It is the body's way of making itself as efficient as possible at performing the task in hand, but at the detriment of lots of other non-essential internal activities. It's the turbo booster in a car, or the afterburner on a fighter aircraft that give extra performance and power, but eat up fuel rapidly and are, therefore, only short-term tools to get you out of immediate danger.

To understand what fear actually is, we need to have an understanding of what causes this feeling.

To have control over our feelings and our fears, we need to be able to recognise the common signs of fear and its effects on our bodies.

Once we can understand and control our own emotions, we can begin to understand how we can manage the same emotions in our potential attackers, and when we know what effects on our bodies these chemicals can have, we recognise the expected effects in our aggressors' bodies, and consequently use that to our advantage.

Just as I'm no NLP guru or knife-fighting expert, nor am I a biologist, so here is my interpretation of what happens to our bodies when experiencing high-stress situations, in simple layman's terms.

## SNS

Within every one of us is an automatic protection system that reacts instinctively to danger. It is controlled by our Sympathetic Nervous System (SNS) which manages the release of the hormone adrenalin into and around our bodies.

Adrenalin raises the level of tension in our muscles so that they are prepared and capable of much greater feats of physical exertion.

In addition, adrenalin increases our heart rate in order to pump more oxygen to help fuel our muscles for this sudden burst of energy, and, depending on the level of threat and the suddenness of your consciously becoming aware of the danger, this can happen incredibly quickly – sometimes, from a resting heart rate of 70 beats per minute to anything up to 170-200 bpm within half a second.

Once the effects of adrenalin are felt in our bodies, this stimulates our emotional feelings and can put us into a state of fear, anger, anxiety or exhilaration, depending on the environment and circumstances.

Adrenalin also has a lot of other physiological effects on our bodies which are all related to our primitive self-preservation system of fight-or-flight. These include the following.

- Diversion of the blood from the extremities such as skin and certain organs such as kidneys, and redirection to the skeletal muscles. This is to ensure that the maximum amount of oxygen reaches the muscles that are going to carry us to safety or help us fight our way out of danger. Some would say that this also helps protect us from blood loss if we are cut or injured during the event, as there is less blood at the peripheral or skin level.
- Our bowel and bladder muscles also tense, which halts the activity of the stomach and gut, as these are not required in

fight-or-flight. This is why you often feel butterflies and nausea in less extreme cases of adrenalin and fearful situations.

- An increase in perspiration, which acts as a preparation to cool the body after the increased activity.
- Tunnel vision is a result of the pupils dilating to try to increase the amount of light entering the eye and also helps us to focus on the main threat. But it is actually a negative by-product in modern conflict as it hinders us from being able to maintain a good spatial awareness and alertness to secondary threats – such as your attacker's friends who are going to blindside you with a bottle over the head perhaps.
- Blood pressure increases as a result of the constriction in blood vessels and increased heart rate.

Each of these side effects or by-products of the release of adrenalin also bring with them their own side effects, some good and some not so good.

There have been lots of studies done on the effects of increased heart rate on the body and the main side effects are below.

- The loss of fine motor skills, such as finger dexterity, and complex hand-to-eye coordination.
- The reduction in complex motor skills, which are three or more gross motor skills being performed in unison, which ultimately leaves us with only gross motor skills. These are the large movements of our primary muscles performing tasks such as running, jumping, etc.
- Dilation of the pupils (of the eyes), which also reduces close-range focus and visual tracking, which is particularly harmful with multiple attackers.
- Increased blood pressure and also the shutting down of part of our brain results in diminished hearing. This is both a physical inability to hear and also a lack of brain activity to store what is heard, so recalling later what was said during the attack can sometimes be difficult.
- The same lack of brain activity in our thinking brain (neocortex) reduces our memory, which is why people will often refer to the event as 'just a blur' and struggle to remember the sequence of events.

- Time distortion also has a major impact and what seems like ages was actually only a few seconds. Often, people talk to me about a fight lasting minutes, when in reality, I am pretty certain it was only a few seconds, 20 to 30 at the very most. I've been trying for a long time to convince my girlfriend of the opposite, and that what appeared to only last for a few seconds was actually hours, but that's a completely different story!

The difficulty lies in trying to introduce these feelings in our training so that we become familiar with the feelings and learn how to work with them and overcome them.

It isn't as simple an act as increasing your heart rate, as it's been proven that an increase in heart rate through exertion does not bring on the same side effects as increased heart rate through adrenalin and fear.

So, in order to become accustomed to these feelings, we have to introduce concepts in our training that bring about stress, anxiety, and fear. We have to engineer our training to be as real as is safely possible in order to trigger these chemicals and then find our own ways of working through it.

Geoff Thompson has covered this particular subject extensively, particularly in his book *Fear – The Friend of Exceptional People* and I would highly recommend you to get this book to learn more about this process and how to become a friend of fear.

What's more important is that all these feelings, emotions and chemical torrents running through your body are also felt in your attacker. They are only human, after all, with the same physiological make-up as your own. Well, perhaps in some cases I would agree we need to use the word 'human' very loosely, and they may also have emerged from the lower end of the gene pool, but you get my point.

Once you have learned what can trigger these emotions in your own body, you can begin to use that knowledge against your attacker.

Ultimately, we are going to switch on massive amounts of adrenalin into our attacker and benefit from all the negative side effects that it brings, such as getting them to freeze with a fight-or-flight response, causing their heart rate to increase rapidly, giving them tunnel vision, nausea, sweating, panic, fear, etc. Or we are going to switch them off and trigger the endorphin release which comes at the end of fight-or-flight and let them relax and think the battle is over, then mount a surprise attack of our own.

Sun Tzu said, *'After the battle, tighten your helmet straps.'* What he wanted his men to do was not to celebrate prematurely and relax, when there may be further attacks ahead.

This is what you are aiming to do with your Submissive Fence: to fool the aggressor into thinking the battle is over and is won, then mount a surprise attack as he begins to celebrate and relax.

## Endorphin Release

Endorphins are chemical painkillers that are produced naturally within the body.

They are a big part of the adrenal process and work hand in hand to help provide analgesic (acting to relieve pain) effects on the body in cases of extreme stress or intense activity.

They help to give the euphoric feeling at the end of a stressful situation, as in any of the thrill-seeking pastimes such as bungee jumping, skydiving, motor racing, etc.

It's widely thought that so-called adrenalin junkies may actually be more addicted to the effects produced by endorphins rather than the adrenalin, and it may also explain how some people are able to withstand incredible injuries and continue to function until they are in safety, such as wounded soldiers in the heat of battle. The painkilling properties coupled with the turbo boost of adrenalin work together to help us escape or continue fighting until the threat has ceased.

Once a high-stress situation is over, such as the end of a battle, the endorphins produce a natural high that will cause you to celebrate and consequently relax, and it is this relaxed state that you can trigger in your aggressor by fooling him the fight is already over, by feigning submission.

In this relaxed state, as has already been mentioned, he will be much more susceptible to a KO from your pre-emptive strike.

The only way to become comfortable, or at least familiar with these feelings is to find ways to immerse yourself in them. Adding realism to your training is one way to achieve this, and is what we did with Animal Day training many years ago.

Animal Day training became widely recognised and made our small martial arts club in Coventry famous overnight for our no-holds-barred, all-out sparring sessions. We would fight with pretty much no rules, any styles, stand-up and ground fighting, until one person won, either with a KO or submission.

While it received mixed reviews for its brutality and violence, there is no doubting that this brought a new element of honesty and realism to our training. It gave us the opportunity to experience fear in all its guises and wallow in it for as long as possible to become more and more desensitised to it.

I'm not saying that this is for everyone, and certainly, my own training and seminars do not contain such types of fighting any more. However, we can find other ways to induce adrenalin and fear throughout our daily lives. All we need to do is look for things that we typically don't enjoy or shy away from and then step in and do them anyway. It may be giving presentations at work that you always manage to avoid, or making cold calls to drum up new business, or putting off that trip to the dentist until you cannot stand the pain any longer.

Grab hold of those things and jump forward to do them before you have to be pushed, because these are the things that will bring on the feelings of fear that you need to become used to. Give it a go.

# Fear: Controlling Your Own Fears

*Listen to what you know, not what you fear.*
—Richard Bach

The most difficult aspect to teach, as a self-defence instructor, is about the effects of fear.

Whilst lots of the effects of adrenalin can be useful in times of physical conflict, the feelings of fear can be debilitating and hinder your application of the Fence strategies.

Probably one of the biggest problems is allowing your adrenalin to bring on a level of fear which pushes you into the freeze state, as this will prevent you from being able to make the necessary decisions to attack first with your pre-emptive strike.

We've already mentioned that one of the common mistakes is to not act quickly enough by failing to throw the first punch, and most of the reasons we fail to do this are related to fear. Below is a list of some of its guises that you need to be aware of.

- Fear of failure: punch not being effective.
- Fear of escalating the situation: antagonising the attacker and making the situation worse.
- Fear of being successful: causing serious injury to the assailant.
- Fear of getting hurt.
- Fear of the unknown: having never hit anyone before.
- Fear of missing the target completely.
- Fear of the aftermath: what happens when the assailant wakes up.
- Fear of being arrested.
- Fear of prison.
- Fear of additional assailants getting involved.
- Fear of how it may be perceived by onlookers.

Notice that these reasons are all based around fear, and many of them are all related to what may happen if you are not successful with your first punch. Missing and/or not knocking the assailant out can result in a lot of consequences which are not all that attractive.

However, these fears are only generated by the stories that you conjure up in your own mind, stories that you quickly script and rehearse in your mind's theatre.

If you are not successful, what can happen?

- You will have to throw additional punches – techniques.
- Fight could/probably will go to the ground.
- Assailant's friends may join in.
- Assailant may become even more aggressive.
- You may/possibly will get hit back.
- You may get injured.
- Your clothes may get damaged (I've lost count of the ripped shirts and torn trousers from scuffles on the door).
- The fight will carry on and you may not be fit enough.
- You stand more chance of being investigated by the police if the fight continues for any length of time.
- More onlookers will gather, drawing more attention, so now you're fighting with a bigger audience.
- You're also fighting with the knowledge that your first shot didn't work, which can be a bit disheartening and also worrying if the guy didn't show any signs of pain from your best shot.

All these things are related to your fear of the unknown, the fear that you have no experience of how effective your own techniques are.

Unfortunately, all the training in the world cannot give you that experience, nor would I suggest you actively go out and *seek* such experience: that would be totally wrong.

So there is always going to be an element of doubt. What we have to do is develop skills to be able to work with and through this doubt and still throw the punch in spite of these feelings.

We can split all these fears into two categories: (1) those which we can deal with and rationalise now, and (2) those which we can only deal with at the moment of conflict.

However, we can train for both now so that, even at the moment of conflict, those feelings aren't as alien as they could be.

Let's take a look at a few of them.

- Fear of escalating the situation: antagonising the attacker and making the situation worse.
- Fear of getting hurt.

There are some schools of thought that say you shouldn't fight back as it can make the situation worse and make the attacker more aggressive. What we have to remember is that our decision to strike pre-emptively should have been based on the fact that we are in honest fear for our safety and that if we don't act we are going to be attacked and/or injured. Therefore, we are already in physical danger, so in my opinion, fighting back cannot make it any worse, but this is my own personal opinion and it is for you to decide what course of action to take. There are no wrong answers with this one: it is a personal choice.

- Fear of how it may be perceived by onlookers.

Who cares?

By this I mean several things.

The vain amongst us may be worried how their techniques will look to those watching.

What I really meant was, how you *think* you will be perceived by those watching: whether they will think you are a bully or totally out of order for hitting someone.

Perhaps they haven't seen the whole situation unfold.

For example, let's say you turned a corner in the high street to see one person on top of another raining punches down on him, how would you know who was in the wrong?

Sure, you may want to stop the guy on top from going overboard and severely hurting the person on the floor, but what if that person had just stabbed the 'attacker's' partner?

I had lots of occasions working the door where customers in the club would be quick to tell me how out of order I was for slapping someone or throwing them out, when they had no idea what had gone on earlier to warrant my actions.

So basically, who cares what people think?

Don't bother as long as you are in the right in your own mind -

it's you who has to sleep easy at night, safe in the knowledge that it was the last resort and you had no other option.

Rationalising these fears now, before any situation ever occurs means they are less likely to reappear during the confrontation.

The fewer the fears and misgivings you have, the fewer decisions you have to make, the more likely you are to not freeze and do what is necessary in a timely manner.

- Fear of additional assailants getting involved.

This is a fear just like any other, but can only be assessed on a situation-by-situation basis.

Depending upon where you are, who's around and the environment, it's difficult to eliminate this fear.

If the guy you're in conflict with has four or five known friends standing right behind him, obviously this has more of an effect on how you will feel than if it was a one-on-one in a dark alley somewhere.

But we can still gain some desensitisation for this kind of feeling by adding it to our training.

Practise sparring with multiple assailants, practise using one assailant as a shield, practise ballooning against lots of people rather than just one attacker.

The more you practise and the more real you can make your training, the less of a debilitating effect this fear will have on you.

- Fear of prison.
- Fear of being arrested.

This one we can definitely eliminate before any situation ever happens.

Remember what we said right at the beginning of this book?

Always be in the right: justification is your ally.

As long as you can say, hand on heart, that you had no other option, that you felt in fear of your life, and that hitting first was the only way you felt you could get out of the situation with your life or without serious personal injury, then you need not be frightened of these two issues.

Inevitably, police involvement will be a factor particularly if you're working in a security industry, when you will always be answerable for your actions. You cannot hit your assailant and then run away: the company you work for will be investigated, etc., etc.

Your attacker may contact the police later and wish to press charges and make a formal complaint.

If you are in a self-protection situation, being attacked/mugged, etc., then it can be slightly different.

You may hit first and then escape – which would always be my first suggestion.

However, you may wish to contact the police yourself and press charges against the attacker.

Certainly, this is one way to get your version of events across to the authorities first, it could mean the difference between you appearing to be the victim or the aggressor.

Ultimately, the only way to get comfortable with dealing with the law and police is to experience it – and I wouldn't advise putting yourself in situations where you are likely to be on the wrong side of a prison cell door!

However, equally, the fact that you should always be in the right and fully justified is a great advantage and should help be a comfort to you; be right and say the right things and the police will be there to help you.

Knowledge is power, which is why I've included a short chapter on the law in order to help eliminate some of these fears now rather than have to worry about the unknown later.

- Fear of the aftermath: what happens when the assailant wakes up.

Sometimes there's no easy way to advise people on how to deal with certain fears.

Sometimes you just have to tell them to suck-it-up a little – toughen up!

This fear is particularly applicable to those in a security-type role where you are often confronted by people who are known to you or your colleagues.

People with reputations or connections that you don't want to get involved with.

I've dealt with people who most certainly scared me with their connections and who I never wanted to fight, purely because I knew they were prepared to go to a level of violence that I was reluctant to go to.

Sometimes this fear can be triggered when you aren't familiar with your assailant, but he has used techniques shown in this book against you.

And here's the key.

They are techniques, that is all; threats and promises of violence to come are merely that. Techniques.

Techniques we can all learn and use, and definitely techniques which you should use, particularly when wanting to back down your opponent.

If there is prolonged dialogue before the situation escalates to becoming physical, you may hear things such as:

'Do you know who I am?'

'I'll come back and do x, y, z to you.'

'I can make one phone call and have a team down here for you.'

Etc., etc., etc.

When we talk about ballooning and you're the one saying these things, ask yourself why you would say them.

It's probably because you're hoping they scare your opponent so that you don't have to fight him. Maybe you're outnumbered or outgunned, or maybe you're scared and want to frighten your opponent with empty promises of exaggerated violence in the hope that they bottle it first.

Well, now tell yourself that this is exactly what your opponent is trying to do to you, and, therefore, he's probably already scared and is hoping his threats frighten you so that it doesn't progress to physical conflict.

They are merely words aimed at trying to invoke a chemical reaction in your body to promote a feeling of fear.

But even if they are true, it doesn't change the situation right at that moment. So what if he brings back a team next week: it won't help him right now. The key to this fear is being able to have a mindset that says, 'Whatever happens, I can deal with it.'

There's no point worrying about something that either will never happen or won't happen for some time.

Deal with the situation in hand and know that all these threats are simply techniques, ones that you already know and ones you are more practised in than him.

# Know Your Enemy

*If you know the enemy and know yourself you need
not fear the results of a hundred battles.*

—Sun Tzu

If we want to enhance our awareness strategies, it helps if we
know what to look for, so it's important that we try to understand
what the common traits are in those likely to attack us.

I'm not suggesting that we learn what is going through our
attackers' minds, what makes them do what they do, because
I'm sure you could find a thousand different reasons for why
certain individuals want to mug, threaten, attack, scare, and
bully good, honest people who just want to get on with their
lives.

However, there are key actions and behaviours that will give
us an early warning of the hostile intentions of these types of
individuals.

These are often referred to as Attack Rituals and are the types
of things you should be looking for when in Code Yellow and
passively alert.

In addition to this, there are certain characteristics and signals
that an attacker will look for in his victim selection process, so
it's also important that you understand these so that you can
ensure you are not displaying the classic signs of a victim.

It's sometimes referred to as Target Hardening and is all based
on knowing what an attacker looks for in potential prey and
ensuring you do not fit in these criteria.

For a deeper look into these two key areas of self-protection
and personal safety, I would highly recommend you read *Dead or
Alive* by Geoff Thompson.

# Attack Rituals

The rituals of an attacker vary depending on the form it takes, from mugging to street robbery, to physical assaults in pubs and clubs, to snatch-and-run thefts, so I will attempt to give only a very generalised overview.

## Locations

This is particularly applicable to street robberies and muggings. Don't be fooled into thinking this will only happen in dark, secluded areas. Whilst these are obviously dangerous places, lots of attacks happen in what feel like busy public areas. This is most likely because, as individuals, we are probably less switched on when walking along a busy high street in the daytime than when walking through a lonely subway at night.

In busy pubs and clubs, whilst muggings and robberies will most likely take place in quiet areas, such as toilets, fights and assaults will happen anywhere.

However, it goes without saying that attackers are going to use their environment to help deliver their assault, whether that be a surprise ambush attack where you are jumped on as you round a corner, or jumped out on from a shop doorway, or to the use of night-time and the cover of darkness to aid their attack.

## Body Language

Most attackers will use eye contact as a primary means of assessing their prey before they go in for attack.

In a mugging scenario, attackers will often walk past their intended victim several times, always looking at them, in order to see if eye contact is returned. If their gaze is not met, it's likely you are switched-off, which is exactly what the attacker is looking for. He will then have the surprise element when he makes his move.

In busy pubs and clubs, eye contact is a way of initiating the attack. The aggressor will stare, wide-eyed, as if challenging you to stare back.

The difficulty with this is, if you stare back equally as long you will probably escalate the situation into verbal, 'What you fecking looking at?' type challenges, whereas, if you look down and avoid the eye contact you may come across as meek and timid, another characteristic the attacker will be looking for.

If the attacker is particularly agitated, you will see lots of signs of adrenalin, such as sucking of the bottom lip, clenching and un-clenching of fists, shoulders back and chest out.

In a crowded place you may see them start to pace a little, moving side to side, with sharp, jerky head movements as if in a heightened state of awareness.

If they are walking, you will see a bounce in their step, arms moving a little more than necessary, and away from their body, as if carrying two rolls of carpet.

This is all their way of making themselves look bigger and more threatening than they are.

With the rise of 'The Hoodie', hiding of faces and becoming anonymous is another way a potential attacker will try to make himself appear more threatening and menacing, and is done merely to play on people's fears.

## Dialogue

Whilst some attacks start with the assailant punching you in the face to gain the immediate upper hand and plunge you straight into the freeze state of adrenalin and fear, a lot of attacks will begin with some form of dialogue.

In street robberies, it's very common for the attacker to use a deceptive approach and be polite and courteous, possibly asking a distractive question such as, 'Do you have the time?' or 'Do you have a light?' or 'Do you know the way to...?'.

This is all done to distract you and engage your brain in an activity or thought process, such as checking your watch or thinking of the best route. Whilst in this momentary distracted state, the attacker will make his move, either pulling out a weapon to threaten you, or punching you or dragging you into a quieter area.

In situations where assault rather than robbery is the motive, such as pubs, clubs, etc., the dialogue will either take the same form, or be aggressive from the outset.

Short, aggressive sentences, threats, challenges, guttural language, these will all be used in an attempt to scare you and bottle you out.

As I said, this is by no means a comprehensive list, but more of a taster of some of the things to look out for in a potential attacker, and things you should be continually assessing when in your alert and aware Code Yellow.

## Victim Selection

Now that we know a little about what to look for in an attacker, we now need to understand what an attacker will look for in us, as potential prey.

A lot of this is base-level body language, and often, an attacker may not consciously realise that he is seeking people with these types of characteristics, however, he will seek them out subconsciously as this tells their intuition that they have picked the right prey, one of which they are more likely to be victorious over.

First, any would-be attacker is looking for an easy target and unless they are clinically insane, they are not going to attack someone that they think is likely to fight back, injure them or make the job more difficult than it already is.

No one wants to fight a monster, which is why the Aggressive Fence and posturing are so effective when done correctly because it makes you into the monster that the attacker no longer wants to risk fighting.

The only time we will fight someone whom we know or feel has the ability to beat us to a pulp, is when we have no other option and/or we need to defend ours and our loved ones lives. Due to the fact that this is all done at a subconscious level on the part of the attacker, the signals we give out with our body language and general demeanour can have a massive bearing on whether we are even selected as the next victim.

Simply being in Code Yellow will cause you to change the way you observe your surroundings, the way you walk, the way you carry yourself, and this alone can dissuade potential attackers from selecting you.

## The Way You Walk

Walk smoothly with confidence. Keep up pace with the flow of traffic (pedestrian traffic – not road traffic!).

Be assertive and deliberate with the direction you take, avoid looking lost or confused, even if you are.

## Posture

The way you carry yourself is vitally important.

You should appear confident and composed, self-assured and in control.

Attackers are looking for people who slouch, who are under-confident, looking at the floor, timid and nervous. They simply want a soft target, one who is not switched on, more likely to be surprised by a sudden attack, and more likely to fall for their deception.

## Eye Contact

Whilst maintaining eye contact for too long can sometimes flare up the situation, avoiding all eye contact by looking down or immediately looking away is a sign of nervousness and will attract further attention from the attacker.

If you are working your Code Yellow awareness well, you are likely to have spotted a potential attacker before he has spotted you. This means you can deliberately avoid any eye contact with this individual but still maintain a confident, head up, assertive posture.

Make eye contact and you need to maintain it to show your confidence. I will often nod or throw a brief smile if eye contact is made which then gives me an opening to move my gaze elsewhere without it seeming too negative or submissive.

## Awareness

Attackers are looking for people in Code White, so by being aware you project an image of vigilance that can not only help you to identify potential threats, but also remove you from the selection pool completely.

## Be Fit

Attackers don't want to fight people who may be able to beat them. Being fit also gives you better body posture, better composure, better fluidity of movement, and can also help you to escape or fight more effectively should you need to.

## Know Yourself, Know Your Enemy

Knowledge is king, and so simply by reading this fantastic book and others like it, you will gain more self-protection awareness and understanding. Without realising it, you will then project this knowledge that will subconsciously be picked up by these Neanderthal individuals who will instinctively remove you from their selection criteria.

# The Fence and the Law

The list of things 'I am not' continues, and here you will notice I am not an expert in the law, but do have an awareness of my legal position as a law-abiding citizen who has the right to defend himself against violent attack and prevent others from causing me, or those around me, injury and harm.

The first point to make would be that we are often hung by what we say, not what we do. Consequently, whilst you may have been fully justified and completely within the law in your self-defence actions, you may still be prosecuted and even found guilty if you come across in your statement with the wrong attitude and say the wrong things.

So the important thing is to first be able to indicate that it was an unprovoked attack, and that you had made it clear you didn't want any trouble. You then need to be able to show or explain how you tried all the options available to you to defuse the situation without the need for violence. After that, you need to be able to honestly say that you still felt under threat, in danger, possibly in fear of your life, and that you had no other option but to strike first in order to prevent personal injury or the injury of other innocent parties nearby.

This is why making statements such as, 'I don't want any trouble,' or asking a distracting question such as, 'Can't we just talk about it?' are great for supporting your case should there be police involvement, as well as engaging your attacker's few brain cells before you bounce them around his cranium with a solid right hook.

Above all, you need to be able to honestly say you had no other option and had to strike first.

The law states that the basic principles of self-defence are:

It is both good law and good sense that a man who is attacked may defend himself. It is both good law and good sense that he may do, but only do, what is reasonably necessary.

Depending on the circumstances, the common law approach may also be applicable (Section 3, Criminal Law Act, 1967):

A person may use such force as is deemed reasonable in the circumstances in the prevention of crime, or in effecting or assisting in the lawful arrest of offenders or suspected offenders or of persons unlawfully at large.

Section 3 applies to the prevention of crime, but there can often be an overlap when dealing with self-defence situations as they may involve some criminal activity on the part of the aggressor, such as breaking into your home or attacking another member of the public, etc.

The key phrase here is the use of *'reasonable force'*. That is a level of force that you deemed to be reasonable under the circumstances.

What the law does recognise, however, is that in cases of self-defence where you may be under extreme duress, you may not have the clarity of thought to consider all the intricacies of what may or may not be deemed reasonable. Effectively, you have a little bit of flexibility here, so you will not be expected to have *precisely analysed* what the minimum level of force will be to resolve the situation.

The burden of proof still remains with the prosecution when the issue of self-defence is raised. It is not your job to prove that you were acting lawfully to defend yourself or another person, and that the force you used was excessive: that is for the prosecution to prove.

However, as you can see, the wording is very grey and every case is treated individually, so what you say at the time of the incident and after the event can have a great deal of bearing on the outcome of any investigation, as a lot of it is subjective and personal.

You are legally allowed to strike pre-emptively (hit first). The law recognises that it is not good self-defence to wait to be attacked physically before you initiate a physical response. It also recognises that you do not need to have been violently attacked yourself in order to lawfully administer a pre-emptive strike or strikes when you see that someone else is in danger of a potentially violent attack.

Where it becomes unlawful is if you are malicious and violent in your attack after the danger has passed, or if you have been premeditated in your attack and laid ambush, or have actively been carrying a weapon in preparation of the possibility of an attack.

If you have actively sought the confrontation rather than tried your best to avoid it, then your subsequent actions will not be seen as lawful.

In my time as a nightclub doorman, I would often knock people out and then place them in a recovery position, or even administer first aid if required. This is something that I was legally obliged to do, and so are you as a civilian, even if I were being attacked by this individual and acting in self-defence.

However, it is also acceptable for you to flee the situation immediately after rendering the attacker unconscious if you feel that remaining there would continue to leave you in danger.

Even so, it is still your responsibility to summon medical assistance for the unconscious or injured attacker once you are safely away.

From a self-defence instructor's perspective, I would always advise making your escape immediately after you have neutralised the threat. Calling medical assistance when you are safely away from the danger would then help to show that you did not want trouble, and that you are a law-abiding citizen who does not want to go around harming people.

## How do We Deem what is Reasonable Force?

This is a very grey area, and whilst there have been quite high-profile cases suggesting the law is in favour of the criminal when it comes to self-defence, for the majority of the cases that reach prosecution, common sense usually prevails.

The legal system will measure your actions and assess whether they were reasonable based on factors including the following.

- The severity of the attack/crime you are trying to prevent.
- Whether you had considered and exhausted all other non-violent means to prevent the attack/crime.
- The relative level of the threat to you as an individual, the size and strength of the attacker, how many attackers there were, what weapons the attacker had, etc.
- Your perception of the threat, and the indication of the level of violence proposed by the attackers.
- Your perceived consequences of defeat.
- Did you cease to attack once the threat was neutralised?
- Under what circumstances did you find yourself in that environment? Was it something you could have avoided completely?

In terms of your own actions, there are certain things which absolutely aren't lawful.

- Carrying weapons, even for self-defence purposes.
- Actively seeking the violent confrontation.
- Failing to make your escape at the earliest opportunity and continuing to attack when the threat is no longer present.
- Using lethal force except as an absolute last resort.

However, all of this aside, in a self-defence situation, your primary goal is to protect yourself, and your main focus should be on self-preservation by whatever means necessary regardless of how it may be interpreted by the law.

Whilst I do not want to spend any time in prison, I prefer much less the prospect of spending the rest of my life 6 ft under because I was too worried about the level of my reasonable force response and not enough about whacking the guy on the head so hard he wakes up with his clothes out of fashion.

Be first, be ferocious, hit as hard as you possibly can, then get out of there.

If you were justified in your actions, and you say the right things when questioned, the law will be on your side.

# How to Escape

If the core concepts of self-protection include awareness, avoidance, and escape, how do we combine our core survival tactics of escape with the Fence?

I think the first thing to remember is that if we are at the stage where we are considering switching from our natural Passive Fence to either a Submissive or Aggressive Fence, then we are already past the point where it is viable and safe to escape. We're already engaged, and should have already made the conscious decision to act in one form or another.

The essence of the Fence is that it puts you in charge of the situation even when you appear outwardly to be the one who is scared and baulking under the fear of your assailant – it is *you* who has decided to act in this manner, and you are doing it for a specific reason.

There is a massive difference between actually being frozen with fear induced by an aggressive or intimidating aggressor, and acting out the same physical symptoms.

To win any situation you have to be the one in charge, and often that can be aided by the fact that you appear the very opposite. How much easier is to get people to do things when they think it was their idea in the first place?

This same philosophy should be remembered when you are creating exits for your assailant once you have backed them down. Give them a way out, but let them think it's *their* idea and that *they* have chosen that action.

No one wants to be told what to do, and even those who do it under duress are not happy and could easily change their mind. However, if you let them think it's their idea, then they are more likely to follow through with the action; that is to say, to leave and thus avoid any conflict.

So to escape, you really need to be doing this earlier, before you're into close-range Fence tactics. If you only consider physical action when you have exhausted all other avenues, then one of those avenues attempted will have been to escape.

First, you should have been aware of your surroundings. Second, you should have avoided any 'dodgy' situations, and if you sense or detect any such untoward situation brewing, then escape should happen at this stage, not later.

Later is too late, just as is waiting to be attacked before you start throwing punches is also too late.

Who cares if you feel silly turning and running from a nightclub or a chip shop or a car park when you start to feel uncomfortable? Who cares what it looks like to the outsider?

More importantly, who cares if it makes you feel cowardly or dents your ego?

At least you're around tomorrow to fix your damaged ego and to have a laugh about it.

Listen to your intuition: if something feels suspicious, it probably is. Don't hang around to try to prove your intuition wrong either by trying to show you're tougher than your intuition thinks, or to show those around you that you're tough enough to be in such places.

Having said all that, escape, or rather, your exit strategies, must still be considered, whether that be how you escape after you have KOd your assailant, or after you have backed him down.

## Escaping After a Submissive Fence

I said earlier that when you are submissive, it is primarily a way to gain an opening for your pre-emptive strike. Therefore, we have to assume that escape after a Submissive Fence is to simply get yourself away from the location after you have successfully dealt with the attacker.

Again, it depends on the situation, your surroundings, onlookers, etc., but one thing I always tried to do when working on the door was to ensure that the now-unconscious attacker was safe after I had dealt with him. This may sound odd, and again, may not be applicable to all situations, but certainly when working the door, if I had no option but to hit someone, I still didn't want them to die on me or end up more injured than was necessary.

So, providing it was safe to do so, I would frequently roll the unconscious attacker into a recovery position, or make sure he had a clear airway and wasn't in any further danger.

Apart from a few occasions, I like to think that I dealt with my aggressors in a compassionate way. For sure, I dealt with them in an extremely violent and efficient way, but always with compassion.

Working the door is a unique environment as you often cannot leave the scene after an altercation. You have the rest of your night shift to work, and if you've hit someone, that could often mean police involvement at some point, and doing your best to help the assailant not only saves you from standing in front of a jury, but also looks good for those eyewitnesses who would have otherwise only seen this aggressive doorman banging innocent punters in the head.

This gives them a contradiction that makes them think there must have been more to the situation than first appears.

If it is a mugging incident or something similar, then escape should just mean getting the hell out of there as quickly as possible, and, being aware in the first place, you should have already assessed your escape routes. This is something you should do on a continuous basis as you walk or drive around.

So from a Submissive Fence, you deal with the assailant with your pre-emptive strike, then you run away. It's as simple as that.

## Escape From Aggressive Fence

This is more complex because we have two forms of escape: either you leave the scene, or your potential attacker(s) leaves the scene.

If you abscond after you've just backed off your attacker, it's very difficult not to appear to have suddenly changed your mind and backed down yourself. Moving away too quickly or in a panic can give your attackers a new lease of life and trigger their own attack rituals again, suddenly giving them the urge to give chase as they now think they're back in charge.

Ballooning and posturing are great ways to hide your escape as they allow you to move away whilst still reinforcing your aggressive stance.

I often used the situation to my advantage, for example, I'd pretend I was suddenly worried about police involvement as a way of justifying my escape.

You have to make your assailant believe that you are leaving the scene for any reason imaginable other than the one that 'you're scared of him', and just as our aggressor may allow his friends to drag him away when he's been defeated with your aggression, likewise, I would allow any of my friends with me to drag me away, under animated duress on my part.

Remember, at this stage your aggressors should be in a position where they want to get away themselves, so, if they think they are being saved by one of your own friends dragging you away, they will be grateful for that. If you've done your job correctly, they will be desperate for you to be gone and out of their lives.

It also allows them to save a little face, because they are still there, and it is you who is leaving; they feel like they now appear to have won to the onlooking public, when in fact they are still petrified inside.

Let your ego go: all you want is for it to end without physical confrontation, so if that means giving them a little room to save face at the end of the confrontation, even better. Leave your ego at home and you'll be safe to join it later.

Your other means of escape is to let your aggressor(s) leave the scene.

Again, even though you've scared the life out of them, it's still a compassionate gesture to let them save a little face when they leave/escape.

So the same techniques apply. Let their friends drag them away; even tell their friends to drag them away. Trust me, every one of them will be secretly glad of the opportunity to be the 'dragger' or 'draggee' if it means getting away from this ferocious monster who has just invaded their lives.

If it's a group of attackers and you've gone through your Aggressive Fence rituals, they will all be looking for a way out, so one way is to bring the aggression back to the lead individual using the isolation techniques.

By telling his friends to take him away, you've done several things.

You've isolated the main aggressor which, by implication, means you have now left out his friends and removed them from your main hit list.

Then you've given them a job to do, which means they can now leave the scene having performed a task, one which actually makes them feel bigger again because they are going to pull away their aggressive friend.

They may look and may even feel like they are doing you the favour and saving you from a hiding that their friend would administer, but subconsciously they know they are simply escaping and saving their friend.

It also gives the main attacker his escape route, and he's happy to let his friends drag him away because it means he can now throw verbal insults and threats at you without the fear that he is going to be allowed to back them up – which of course, he is now very worried about having to do.

I've had lots of situations where a large male aggressor has been sufficiently backed-down with my aggressive posturing that his girlfriend of half his size has been able to drag him away.

A good friend of mine working the door was always fond of shouting, 'If you can't get past your girlfriend, you don't scare me,' which was sometimes not a great idea because it would flare the situation up again, but it was nonetheless very true.

I've even seen occasions where the friends have either deliberately or accidentally let go of their lead attacker friend only to have him remain in the 'I'm being dragged away against my will' position. Arms back, leaning forward, but not actually moving forward.

Again, the key here is to let them save face.

Once you sense that the violent confrontation is reaching a resolution, it's very easy to celebrate early, maybe throw the odd snide comment at your departing attackers, try to gain a bit more admiration from your onlookers by your cool humour. However, it can be a mistake and can often reignite the fuse of your attackers, and then you've got a problem all over again.

This is ego again – and it has to be kept in check.

# Training the Fence

As with everything, repetition is the key to becoming good at Fence Concepts and the techniques contained in this manual.

The more you drill these principles, the more likely they are going to be absorbed in your subconscious and be available to you when you need them most.

We have already spoken about commentary techniques that you can practise to help ensure you remain in Code Yellow and not drift back into wide-asleep Code White. The next step is then to train the various Fence positions, ideally with one or more partners.

The Passive Fence is something that you should practise continually throughout your waking hours. It should be with you all the time, and is something that you can play with when standing and talking to friends to see if they notice your hand movements and control of personal space.

In the gym, you can practise all variations of the Fence with a partner. Have your partner role-play with you, and no, I don't mean have them dress up in a nurse's outfit, as appealing as that may be.

Get your partner to act as the aggressor, start becoming hostile, pushing, shoving, prodding, throwing verbal insults while you then work on maintaining your control, keeping your personal space, and using the Controlling Fence.

Remember, when training this technique, you can make this scenario last for 10 or 20 or 30 seconds so that you can practise keeping space and control. In reality, this would only be for one or two seconds, then you're looking at taking steps to bring this confrontation to a conclusion.

With more than one partner, you can start to work multiple-attacker role-plays, and again, this enables you to monitor more than one target with your Controlling Fence, practise your explosive shove or kicks into an Aggressive Fence, etc.

If the role-playing feels unnatural or uncomfortable and you don't enjoy doing it, good. That is a readymade exercise for you to experience mild adrenalin and discomfort and something that you should embrace and drill until it does become comfortable.

## Training on Your Own

When training on your own, the best equipment to use is the punch bag.

I continually work on my pre-emptive striking techniques on a good, heavy punch bag.

The key to this training is to treat each punch or kick as an independent attack and avoid getting into a rhythm that will gradually speed up and up until you are almost throwing a slow combination of punches rather than single KO blows.

Stand in front of the bag, maintain your distance using your Fence positions, practise your dialogue, ask your question, then launch your strike.

You may get a few funny looks in the gym if you start asking the punch bag, 'Can't we just talk about it?' but do it anyway. You need to drill these techniques in the same way you expect to use them for real.

So, remember your timing and make sure you leave a brief pause between your question and your strike.

## Training with a Single Partner

(Or training with a married partner – it works just the same.)

Focus pads are the best equipment for drilling and training your pre-emptive strikes.

Refer back to the lists of attacks in the 'Attacks from the Fence' chapter, and drill each one repeatedly until you find the best strikes for you, the ones with which you feel most comfortable and natural.

Drill each technique from the different Fence positions so that you learn how to punch with your hands starting in a low (passive) position, up to a very high, close-range (submissive) position, as shown in Pictures 47a and 47b.

It's the responsibility of your partner holding the pads to ensure that they keep them at a realistic height, and apply forward pressure with the pad as you strike in order to give you some positive feedback to your punch, which gives you the feeling of weight behind your punch, and can also help prevent injury from hyper-extension of your joints.

Remember to treat your attacks as one single punch, always returning to your chosen Fence position before attacking again so as not to get into bad habits that can see you gradually returning to your more natural guard position, if you are a boxer, for example.

Pictures 47a                                     Pictures 47b

An important thing to notice with all of these training techniques is that your distancing needs to be adjusted so that you are at the correct distance from the *pad*, and not necessarily the pad-*holder*.

The pad is now your intended target, i.e. the jaw, so you have to assume the rest of the attacker's body is in that position too.

Use the spot on the focus pad as the target and aim to hit this every time, as shown in Pictures 48a and 48b.

Picture 48a                              Picture 48b

From a slightly closer range, angle the pad downwards for uppercuts.

Hand positions can be conventional with palms facing in towards you or palms facing more to the side, thus reducing the amount of twisting of the hand for a more direct approach to the target, as shown in Pictures 49a and 49b.

Picture 49a                              Picture 49b

With the distance much less, you can train elbows on the pads, as shown in Picture 50.

Depending on what styles you've trained in the past, you may prefer to cover with your opposite hand, but this again is personal preference.

The main aim of this manual is to show you how these strikes fit in with the Fence Positions, and not actually teach you the strikes.

Restrictive punching on the pads is a great way to develop explosive power without the need for big build-ups before the punch, which can often telegraph the shot, causing the aggressor to flinch and tense up before you make contact.

Picture 50

Picture 51a                                    Picture 51b

One way to achieve this in padwork is to have your pad-holder use his free hand to prevent you from recoiling before you punch, as can be seen here in Pictures 51a and 51b, with a close-range right hook, which has to be thrown directly from the Fence Position without any body rotation to the right prior to the punch.

Remember to train everything from both sides, so if you practise a right hook off the back hand, i.e. your left foot is slightly forward, remember to switch this and try a left hook with your right foot forward.

While our intention is to use the Fence Concepts to help disguise our movements and preparations to attack, we are often not blessed with a comfortable, 'preferred' position and have to be

Picture 52a                              Picture 52b

able to deliver KO blows from any angle or position, such as in Pictures 52a, 52b, and 52c.

Slaps, particularly off a lead hand are excellent, especially when coupled with a questioning-type Fence.

Again, using the pad-holder to give restriction to your movement, you can train your lead hand slaps and hooks with limited

Picture 52c

movement, as can be seen in Pictures 53a and 53b.

Picture 53a                    Picture 53b

Most importantly, always try to make sure your pad-holder is focused on what you are doing, so that he can prepare for the power of your shot as it connects with the pad, rather than posing for the camera.

And if all else fails, scare them off with 'milk-bottle white' legs, something Mick and I have been perfecting for many years.

I have spent thousands of hours hitting

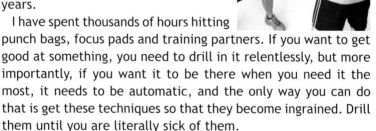

punch bags, focus pads and training partners. If you want to get good at something, you need to drill in it relentlessly, but more importantly, if you want it to be there when you need it the most, it needs to be automatic, and the only way you can do that is get these techniques so that they become ingrained. Drill them until you are literally sick of them.

Pick one or two favourite techniques, and, to coin a phrase, Make It Your Own.

Above all, have fun!

# Epilogue

If you've made it this far, then I thank you for sticking with this book, my first full instructional training manual.

The Fence and all its concepts are a personal thing. All I have been able to do in this text is show you some examples of how I use it and how others I have trained and worked with also use it.

However, as with all martial arts – indeed, anything in life – what fits one person will not fit everyone. So it is with this in mind that I urge you to start training the Fence Concepts and find your own way using the techniques I have shown as a skeleton or building blocks for you to create your own structure.

Train it so much that it becomes natural. Code Yellow and Passive Fence should be a way of life and not something you try to put into action when the need arises.

Listen to your intuition. You are all blessed with an invisible in-built self-protection mechanism that will always know when something is wrong or when you are making the wrong decision. Listen to it, and have the confidence and self-control to act on it.

Develop the self-control to override your ego, because ego will get you into trouble and force you further up the Fence Concepts Flowchart into the Code Orange and Code Red areas, where you don't want to be.

If you are training in any reality-based martial arts and not training the Fence, then you are missing the most important part of self-protection, in my humble opinion, and if you take only one lesson away from this book it is this:

*Stay alert, stay switched on, and practise avoidance wherever possible.*

If all else fails and you can no longer escape, then use your Fence techniques to disguise your intentions and hit first. Be ferocious, hit as hard as you possibly can, and do not stop until there is no longer a threat. Then get away quickly and safely.

I thank you all for reading this book, and wish you all the very best in your training endeavours.

Stay Safe and Have Fun.

Al Peasland
August 2008

# Thank You

I would like to take this opportunity to send massive thanks to all those who have helped me create this book, with special thanks to:

- Geoff and Sharon Thompson, for their guidance, support and encouragement, and a fantastic foreword. Thanks for always being there and for showing me I can achieve absolutely anything I want.
  www.geoffthompson.com
- Tony Leach, for all his branding and artwork assistance and tireless patience with my constant stream of 'shit sandwiches'. I definitely couldn't have done all of this without you, so a massive, massive thanks.
- To Robert Hipgrave and Matt Richards for your amazing generosity and support and for turning Tony's artwork into glossy reality.
- Tony Papps of TP Photography, for the photographs in this book and other promotional material. Thanks for your creative assistance and for keeping me in focus.
  tony.papps@btinternet.com
  http://papps.smugmug.com
- Peter Skillen of Mr Tees Sports and Fightwear Branding, for the T-shirts and training gear on the accompanying Fence Concepts DVD.
  peter_mrtees@hotmail.co.uk
- To Dhiren Bahl of WordsWay Copyediting, for doing an excellent job of copy-editing and typesetting my scrawl and for the constant professionalism. Many Thanks.
  www.WordsWay.com
  dhirenbahl@vsnl.com
- To Tricia Cunningham for her superb Fence demonstration on the cover of the book and DVD. Thanks for your help and for the great QT.
- Last but not least, thanks to my brother Mick Tully for his assistance with this book and DVD, for being a great training partner and coach, and for being a top mate and general all-round good guy. Keep up the positivity.

# AL PEASLAND 自
## COMPLETE SELF PROTECTION

Complete Self-Protection offers training in self-defence techniques and concepts that enable you to protect yourself and your loved ones in the increasingly violent society we all live in.

Whether you want to:

- increase your physical self-defence skills;
- improve your general fitness levels;
- find a fun way to learn martial arts;
- use this training to improve your motivation; or
- realise your true potential;

...CSP has something for you.

CSP offers self-protection training in the following formats:
- Private instruction – female instructors available.
- Regular martial arts classes.
- Group and corporate seminars.
- Women-only seminars.

## www.CompleteSelfProtection.com

Tel: 07967 000 282          Email: info@alpeasland.com

# BUY FENCE CONCEPTS ON DVD - NOW

As an excellent accompaniment to the Fence Concepts Book, that I hope you have enjoyed reading, you can now purchase the Fence Concepts DVD.

The DVD takes the words and illustrations from this book and brings them to life, showing how all the various stages of the 'Fence' work in real time whilst demonstrating the power of effective pre-emptive striking.

# FENCE CONCEPTS – DVD
## Price £19.99

Over an hour of instruction, plus bonus interview and Geoff Thompson Masterclass Promo Footage.

There are lots and lots of people teaching pre-emptive striking these days. But who better to learn it from than Geoff Thompson's longest-serving instructor, Al Peasland?

In the Fence Concepts DVD, Al takes you step by step through the logic behind the application of the 'Fence'. In his own words, Al considers these concepts to be the most fundamental tool in any reality-based self-defence system.

· Learn how to gain the upper hand in any aggressive and violent confrontation.

· Learn how to defuse situations simply by controlling the adrenaline and emotions in your potential attacker.

· And when things really go bad, learn how to use devastating strikes and attacks to end the conflict with a single technique.

This DVD is a must-see for everyone who is serious about learning to defend themselves – trained martial artists or not!

For more details, please check out Al's Complete Self Protection website:

### www.CompleteSelfProtection.com

## Fence Concepts DVD Reviews

I'd like to send special thanks to the gentlemen listed below who have been kind enough to critique the Fence Concepts DVD and take the time to pen their reviews below.

**Terry Barnett**
*www.integratedarts.co.uk*

*Al Peasland was kind enough to give me a review copy of the first DVD to be released under his CSP banner which covers 'The Fence' concept; I think you will find it a valuable addition to your library.*

*Drawing on both his personal experience, and that of respected colleagues, Al intelligently presents the material which covers the psychology and physiology of potential and actual violent encounters.*

*Whilst at no time glorifying matters, Al takes you step by step through the escalating situations that can occur and presents well-established strategies for dealing with them.*

**Warren Jones**
**Urban Safety**
*www.urbansafety.co.uk*

*As a former police officer and police self-defence instructor, I have spent a considerable amount of time reviewing various systems of self-defence. Having watched this DVD, I would recommend it to anyone with an interest in developing their self-protection skills, including police officers and door supervisors.*

*The DVD is delivered by Alan Peasland who is a highly experienced door supervisor and self-defence instructor. It focuses on how to create a reactionary gap and the training strategies associated with pre-emptive striking. It also discusses fear control and states of awareness. The techniques are proven strategies employed by those who work in violent environments, because they are simple to perform and have a high success rate when delivered in stressful situations. Production is of a high quality and I would recommend it to anyone who is serious about personal safety.*

**Iain Abernethy**
*www.iainabernethy.com*

*Alan Peasland is one of the UK's leading self-protection and practical martial arts instructors. I watched Alan's latest DVD this week and I highly recommend it to everyone on this list! The DVD covers the 'Fence' and Alan breaks down all aspects of this vitally important self-protection concept in a very thorough, structured and accessible way. If you think you understand what the fence is all about, you need to watch this DVD!*